# *The* Uniform Limited Partnership Act *of* 2008

Text, Drafters' Comments,
and Correlation Tables

**CEB Attorney Editor**
Jean Magistrale

CONTINUING EDUCATION OF THE BAR ▪ CALIFORNIA
Oakland, California
For update information call 1-800-232-3444
Website: ceb.com

BU-33919

Library of Congress Catalog No. 2008922519

ISBN 978-0-7626-1366-3
BU-33919

## CONTINUING EDUCATION OF THE BAR • CALIFORNIA

# CEB Governing Committee

# Contents

# Preface

The Uniform Limited Partnership Act of 2008 (known as Re-RUL-PA), operative January 1, 2008, is a major revision of California limited partnership law, designed to govern limited partnerships through one cohesive body of law. The California business law practitioner should have an understanding of the Act's provisions and how they affect existing and newly formed limited partnerships. This publication is intended to assist the practitioner by providing two convenient resources:

- The text of the law as enacted, along with extensive comments prepared by the Drafting Committee of the Partnerships and Limited Liabilities Committee of the Business Law Section of the State Bar of California; and

- Correlation tables showing correlations between old limited partnership law and the new Act, as well as correlations between the new law and old law.

This pamphlet is designed for use with Advising California Partnerships (3d ed Cal CEB 1999). Its contents are current through March, 2010, when CEB plans to incorporate them into a new edition of Advising California Partnerships. CEB would like to extend its deepest gratitude to Phillip L. Jelsma, of Luce Forward Hamilton Scripps LLP, San Diego, for his assistance in developing it.

CEB Attorney Editor Jean Magistrale and Legal Editor Kristin Schwaighart contributed to this title. Laura Linden handled copyediting and production.

## About the Drafting Committee

The Drafting Committee of the Partnerships and Limited Liabilities Committee (PLLC) of the Business Law Section of the State Bar of California was headed by Phillip L. Jelsma, who was chair of the PLLC in 2003–2004. To draft California's Uniform Limited Partnership Act of 2008, the Drafting Committee reviewed the national Uniform Limited Partnership Act, proposed certain amendments to conform to principles of California law, prepared the California Code Comments, and shepherded the Act through the legislative process. It was passed by the Legislature and signed by the Governor on September 27, 2006.

Members of the PLLC Drafting Committee included Richard Burt, Bruce Denning, Edward Gartenberg, Stephen D. Halper, Steven K. Hazen, Jack Johal, David Marion, Charles E. McKee, Joanne S. Rocks, K. Bradley Rogerson, Daniel K. Winton, and Michael Yoon. Others who made valuable contributions include Betsy Bogart of the California Department of Corporations; Tiffany E. Conklin of California state Senator Tom Harman's office; Larry Doyle of the California State Bar's Office of Governmental Affairs; and Pam Giarrizo of the California Secretary of State's office.

Michael Fenger
*Practice Group Manager*
*Business Law*

Pamela J. Jester
*Director*

# THE UNIFORM LIMITED PARTNERSHIP ACT OF 2008, WITH CALIFORNIA CODE COMMENTS AND UNIFORM LIMITED PARTNERSHIP ACT COMMENTS

## UNIFORM LIMITED PARTNERSHIP ACT (2008)

### ARTICLE 1.
### GENERAL PROVISIONS

**SECTION 15900. SHORT TITLE.** This chapter may be cited as the Uniform Limited Partnership Act of 2008.

### California Code Comment
*By Phil Jelsma*

The Drafting Committee of the Partnerships and Limited Liability Companies Committee of the Business Law Section of the State Bar of California relied on Official Comments to the Uniform Limited Partnership Act ( the "Act") in drafting a California version of the Act and noted the differences between the Uniform Act and the California version. The Uniform Limited Partnership Act Comments have been modified to refer to the relevant sections in the California version of the Act.

**SECTION 15901.02. DEFINITIONS.** In this chapter, the following terms have the following meanings:

(a) "Acknowledged" means that an instrument is either of the following: (1) Formally acknowledged as provided in Article 3 (commencing with Section 1180) of Chapter 4 of Title 4 of Part 4 of Division 2 of the Civil Code. (2) Executed to include substantially the following wording preceding the signature: It is hereby declared that I am the person who executed this instrument, which execution is my act and deed.

Any certificate of acknowledgment taken without this state before a notary public or a judge or clerk of a court of record having an official seal need not be further authenticated.

1

(b) "Certificate of limited partnership" means the certificate required by Section 15902.01. The term includes the certificate as amended or restated.

(c) "Contribution" except in the phrase "right of contribution," means any benefit provided by a person to a limited partnership in order to become a partner or in the person's capacity as a partner.

(d) "Debtor in bankruptcy" means a person that is the subject of:

(1) an order for relief under Title 11 of the United States Code or, a comparable order under a successor statute of general application; or (2) a comparable order under federal, state, or foreign law governing insolvency.

(e) "Designated office" means: (1) with respect to a limited partnership, the office that the limited partnership is required to designate and maintain under Section 15901.14; and (2) with respect to a foreign limited partnership, its principal office.

(f) "Distribution" means a transfer of money or other property from a limited partnership to a partner in the partner's capacity as a partner or to a transferee on account of a transferable interest owned by the transferee.

(g) "Domestic corporation" means a corporation formed under the laws of this state.

(h) "Electronic transmission by the partnership" means a communication that meets both of the following requirements: (1) It is delivered by any of the following means: (A) Facsimile transmission or electronic mail when directed to the facsimile number or electronic mail address, respectively, for the recipient on the record with the partnership. (B) Posting on an electronic message board or other electronic database that the partnership has designated for the communication, together with a separate notice to the recipient of the posting, which shall be validly delivered upon the later of either the posting or delivery of the separate notice thereof. (C) Other means of electronic communication. (2) It is to a recipient that has provided an unrevoked consent to the use of the means of transmission used by the partnership in the electronic transmission.

(i) "Electronic transmission to the partnership" means a communication that meets both of the following requirements: (1) It is delivered by any of the following means: (A) Facsimile communication or other electronic mail when directed to the facsimile number or electronic mail address, respectively, that the partnership has provided from time to time to the partners for sending communications to the partnership. (B) Posting on an electronic message board or electronic database that the partnership has designated for the communication. A transmission shall have been validly delivered upon the posting. (C) Other means of electronic communication. (2) It is a communication as to which the partnership has placed in effect reasonable measures to verify that the sender is the partner purporting to send the transmission, either in person or by proxy.

(j) "Foreign limited liability limited partnership" means a foreign limited partnership whose general partners have limited liability for the obligations of the foreign limited partnership.

(k) "Foreign limited partnership" means a partnership formed under the laws of a jurisdiction other than this state and required by those laws to have one or more general partners and one or more limited partners. The term includes a foreign limited liability limited partnership.

(l) "Foreign other business entity" means an other business entity formed under the laws of any state other than this state or under the laws of a foreign country.

(m) "General partner" means:

(1) with respect to a limited partnership, a person that:

(A) becomes a general partner under Section 15904.01 or subdivision (g) of 15907.02; or

(B) was a general partner in a limited partnership when the limited partnership became subject to this chapter under subdivision (a) or (b) of Section 15912.06; and

(2) with respect to a foreign limited partnership, a person that has rights, powers, and obligations similar to those of a general partner in a limited partnership.

(n) "Interests of all partners" means the aggregate interests of all partners in the current profits derived from business operations of the partnership.

(o) "Interests of limited partners" means the aggregate interests of all limited partners in their respective capacities as limited partners in the current profits derived from business operations of the partnership.

(p) "Limited partner" means:

(1) with respect to a limited partnership, a person that:

(A) becomes a limited partner under Section 15903.01; or

(B) was a limited partner in a limited partnership when the limited partnership became subject to this chapter under subdivision (a) or (b) of Section 15912.06; and

(2) with respect to a foreign limited partnership, a person that has rights, powers, and obligations similar to those of a limited partner in a limited partnership.

(q) "Limited partnership" or "domestic limited partnership", except in the phrases "foreign limited partnership" and "foreign limited liability limited partnership," means an entity, having one or more general partners and one or more limited partners, which is formed under this chapter by two or more persons or becomes subject to this chapter under Article 11 (commencing with Section 15911.01) or subdivisions (a) or (b) of Section 15912.06.

(r) "Mail" means first-class mail, postage prepaid, unless registered mail is specified. Registered mail includes certified mail.

(s) "Majority in interest of all partners" means more than 50 percent of the interests of all partners.

(t) "Majority in interest of the limited partners" means more than 50 percent of the interests of limited partners.

(u) "Other business entity" means a corporation, general partnership, limited liability company, business trust, real estate investment trust, or an unincorporated association other than a nonprofit association, but excludes a limited partnership.

(v) "Parent" of a limited partnership means any of the following: (1) A general partner of the limited partnership. (2) A person possessing, directly or indirectly, the power to direct or cause the direction of the management and policies of a general partner of the limited partnership. (3) A person owning, directly or indirectly, limited partnership interests possessing more than 50 percent of the aggregate voting power of the limited partnership.

(w) "Partner" means a limited partner or general partner.

(x) "Partnership agreement" means the partners' agreement, whether oral, implied, in a record, or in any combination, concerning the limited partnership. The term includes the agreement as amended.

(y) "Person" means an individual, partnership, limited partnership, trust, estate, association, corporation, limited liability company, or other entity whether domestic or foreign.

(z) "Person dissociated as a general partner" means a person dissociated as a general partner of a limited partnership.

(aa) "Principal office" means the office where the principal executive office of a limited partnership or foreign limited partnership is located, whether or not the office is located in this state.

(ab) "Proxy" means a written authorization signed by a partner or the partner's attorney in fact giving another person the power to vote with respect to the interest of that partner. "Signed," for the purpose of this subdivision, means the placing of the partner's name on the proxy, whether by manual signature, typewriting, telegraphic transmission, or otherwise by the partner or the partner's attorney in fact.

(ac) "Record" means information that is inscribed on a tangible medium or that is stored in an electronic or other medium and is retrievable in perceivable form.

(ad) "Required information" means the information that a limited partnership is required to maintain under Section 15901.11.

(ae) "Return of capital" means any distribution to a partner to the extent that the aggregate distributions to that partner do not exceed that partner's contributions to the partnership.

(af) "Sign" means:

(1) to execute or adopt a tangible symbol with the present intent to authenticate a record; or

(2) to attach or logically associate an electronic symbol, sound, or process to or with a record with the present intent to authenticate the record.

(ag) "State" means a state of the United States, the District of Columbia, Puerto Rico, the United States Virgin Islands, or any territory or insular possession subject to the jurisdiction of the United States.

(ah) "Time a notice is given or sent," unless otherwise expressly provided, means any of the following: (1) The time a written notice to a partner or the limited partnership is deposited in the United States mail. (2) The time any other written notice is personally delivered to the recipient, is delivered to a common carrier for transmission, or actually transmitted by the person giving the notice by electronic means to the recipient. (3) The time any oral notice is communicated, in person or by telephone or wireless, to the recipient or to a person at the office of the recipient who the person giving the notice has reason to believe will promptly communicate it to the recipient.

(1) "Transact intrastate business" means for purposes of registration, entering into repeated and successive transactions of business in this state, other than interstate or foreign commerce.

(2) A foreign limited partnership shall not be considered to be transacting intrastate business within the meaning of paragraph (1) solely because of its status as one or more of the following:

(A) A shareholder of a foreign corporation transacting intrastate business.

(B) A shareholder of a domestic corporation.

(C) A limited partner of a foreign limited partnership transacting intrastate business.

(D) A limited partner of a domestic limited partnership.

(E) A member or manager of a foreign limited liability company transacting intrastate business.

(F) A member or manager of a domestic limited liability company.

(3) Without excluding other activities that may not constitute transacting intrastate business, a foreign limited partnership shall not be considered to be transacting intrastate business within the meaning of paragraph (1) solely by reason of carrying on in this state one or more of the following activities:

(A) Maintaining or defending any action or suit or any administrative or arbitration proceeding, or effecting the settlement thereof or the settlement of claims and disputes.

(B) Holding meetings of its partners or carrying on other activities concerning its internal affairs.

(C) Maintaining bank accounts.

(D) Maintaining offices or agencies for the transfer, exchange, and registration of its securities or depositories with relation to its securities.

(E) Effecting sales through independent contractors.

(F) Soliciting or procuring orders, whether by mail or through employees or agents or otherwise, where the orders require acceptance without this state before becoming binding contracts.

(G) Creating or acquiring evidences of debt or mortgages, liens, or security interests on real or personal property.

(H) Securing or collecting debts or enforcing mortgages and security interests in property securing the debts.

(I) Conducting an isolated transaction completed within a period of 180 days and not in the course of a number of repeated transactions of like nature.

(J) Transacting business in interstate commerce.

(4) A person shall not be deemed to be transacting intrastate business in this state within the meaning of paragraph (1) solely because

of the person's status as a limited partner of a domestic limited partnership or a foreign limited partnership registered to transact intrastate business in this state. This definition shall not apply in determining the contacts or activities that may subject a foreign limited partnership to service of process, taxation, jurisdiction, or other regulation under any other law of this state.

(ai) "Transfer" includes an assignment, conveyance, deed, bill of sale, lease, mortgage, creation of a security interest or encumbrance, gift, and transfer by operation of law.

(aj) "Transferable interest" means a partner's right to receive distributions.

(ak) "Transferee" means a person to which all or part of a transferable interest has been transferred, whether or not the transferor is a partner.

## Uniform Limited Partnership Act Comment

This section contains definitions applicable throughout the chapter. Section 15911.01 provides additional definitions applicable within Article 11.

**Paragraph (m) [General partner]**—A partnership agreement may vary Section 15904.01 and provide a process or mechanism for becoming a general partner which is different from or additional to the rules stated in that section. For the purposes of this definition, a person who becomes a general partner pursuant to a provision of the partnership agreement becomes a general partner under Section 15912.06.

**Paragraph (p) [Limited partner]**—The Comment to Paragraph (m) applies here as well. For the purposes of this definition, a person who becomes a limited partner pursuant to a provision of the partnership agreement becomes a limited partner under Section 15903.01.

**Paragraph (q) [Limited Partnership]**—This definition pertains to what is commonly termed a "domestic" limited partnership. The definition encompasses: (i) limited partnerships originally formed under this chapter, including limited partnerships formed under Section 15903.01(b) to be the surviving organization in a merger; (ii) any entity that becomes subject to this chapter by converting into a limited partnership under Article 11; (iii) any preexisting domestic limited partnership that elects pursuant to Section 15912.06 to become subject to this chapter; and (iv) all other preexisting domestic limited partnerships when they become subject to this chapter under Section 15912.06.

Following the approach of predecessor law, RULPA Section 101(7), this definition contains two substantive requirements. First, it is of the essence of a limited partnership to have two classes of partners. Accordingly, under Section 15901.02(q), a limited partnership must have at least one general and one limited partner. Section 15908.01 provides that a limited partnership dissolves if its sole general partner or sole limited partner dissociates and the limited partnership fails to admit a replacement within 90 days of the dissociation. The 90-day limitation is a default rule, but, in light of Section 15901.02(q), a limited partnership may not indefinitely delay "having one or more general partners and one or more limited partners."

It is also of the essence of a limited partnership to have at least two partners. Section 15901.02(q) codifies this requirement by referring to a limited partnership as "an entity . . . which is formed under this [chapter] by two or more persons." Thus, while the same person may be both a general and limited partner, Section 15901.13 (Dual Capacity), one person alone cannot be the "two persons" contemplated by this definition. However, nothing in this definition prevents two closely affiliated persons from satisfying the two-person requirement.

**Paragraph (x) [Partnership agreement]**—Section 15901.10 is essential to understanding the significance of the partnership agreement. See also Section 15902.01(d) (resolving inconsistencies between the certificate of limited partnership and the partnership agreement).

**Paragraph (ai) [Transfer]**—Following RUPA, this chapter uses the words "transfer" and "transferee" rather than the words "assignment" and "assignee." See RUPA Section 503.

The reference to "transfer by operation of law" is significant in connection with Section 15907.02 (Transfer of Partner's Transferable Interest). That section severely restricts a transferee's rights (absent the consent of the partners), and this definition makes those restrictions applicable, for example, to transfers ordered by a family court as part of a divorce proceeding and transfers resulting from the death of a partner.

**Paragraph (ak) [Transferee]**—See comment to Paragraph (ii) for an explanation of why this chapter refers to "transferee" rather than "assignee."

## SECTION 15901.03. KNOWLEDGE AND NOTICE.

(a) A person knows a fact if the person has actual knowledge of it.

(b) A person has notice of a fact if the person:

(1) knows of it;

(2) has received a notification of it;

(3) has reason to know it exists from all of the facts known to the person at the time in question; or

(4) has notice of it under subdivision (c) or (d).

(c) A certificate of limited partnership on file in the office of the Secretary of State is notice that the partnership is a limited partnership and the persons designated in the certificate as general partners are general partners. Except as otherwise provided in subdivision (d), the certificate is not notice of any other fact.

(d) A person has notice of:

(1) another person's dissociation as a general partner, 90 days after the effective date of an amendment to the certificate of limited partnership which states that the other person has dissociated or 90 days after the effective date of a certificate of dissociation pertaining to the other person, whichever occurs first;

(2) a limited partnership's dissolution, 90 days after the effective

date of an amendment to the certificate of limited partnership stating that the limited partnership is dissolved;

(3) a limited partnership's termination, 90 days after the effective date of a certificate of cancellation;

(4) a limited partnership's conversion under Article 11 (commencing with Section 15911.01), 90 days after the effective date of the certificate of conversion; or

(5) a merger under Article 11 (commencing with Section 15911.01), 90 days after the effective date of the certificate of merger.

(e) A person notifies or gives a notification to another person by taking steps reasonably required to inform the other person in ordinary course, whether or not the other person learns of it.

(f) A person receives a notification when the notification:

(1) comes to the person's attention; or

(2) is delivered at the person's place of business or at any other place held out by the person as a place for receiving communications.

(g) Except as otherwise provided in subdivision (h), a person other than an individual knows, has notice, or receives a notification of a fact for purposes of a particular transaction when the individual conducting the transaction for the person knows, has notice, or receives a notification of the fact, or in any event when the fact would have been brought to the individual's attention if the person had exercised reasonable diligence. A person other than an individual exercises reasonable diligence if it maintains reasonable routines for communicating significant information to the individual conducting the transaction for the person and there is reasonable compliance with the routines. Reasonable diligence does not require an individual acting for the person to communicate information unless the communication is part of the individual's regular duties or the individual has reason to know of the transaction and that the transaction would be materially affected by the information.

(h) A general partner's knowledge, notice, or receipt of a notification of a fact relating to the limited partnership is effective immediately as knowledge of, notice to, or receipt of a notification by the limited partnership, except in the case of a fraud on the limited partnership committed by or with the consent of the general partner. A limited partner's knowledge, notice, or receipt of a notification of a fact relating to the limited partnership is not effective as knowledge of, notice to, or receipt of a notification by the limited partnership.

## Uniform Limited Partnership Act Comment

**Source**-RUPA Section 102; RULPA Section 208.

Notice and the relationship among subdivisions (b), (c) and (d)-These subdivisions provide separate and independent avenues through which a person can have notice of a fact. A person has notice of a fact as soon as any of the avenues applies.

Example: A limited partnership dissolves and amends its certificate of limited partnership to indicate dissolution. The amendment is effective on March 1. On March 15, Person #1 has reason to know of the dissolution and therefore has "notice" of the dissolution under Section 15901.03(b)(3) even though Section 15901.03(d)(2) does not yet apply. Person #2 does not have actual knowledge of the dissolution until June 15. Nonetheless, under Section 15901.03(d)(2) Person #2 has "notice" of the dissolution on May 30.

**Subsection (c)**—This subdivision provides what is commonly called constructive notice and comes essentially verbatim from RULPA Section 208. As for the significance of constructive notice "that the partnership is a limited partnership," see *Water, Waste & Land, Inc. v Lanham* (Colo 1998) 955 P2d 997, 1001-1003 (interpreting a comparable provision of the Colorado LLC statute and holding the provision ineffective to change common law agency principles, including the rules relating to the liability of an agent that transacts business for an undisclosed principal).

As for constructive notice that "the persons designated in the certificate as general partners are general partners," Section 15902.01(a)(3) requires the initial certificate of limited partnership to name each general partner, and Section 15902.02(b) requires a limited partnership to promptly amend its certificate of limited partnership to reflect any change in the identity of its general partners. Nonetheless, it will be possible, albeit improper, for a person to be designated in the certificate of limited partnership as a general partner without having become a general partner as contemplated by Section 15904.01. Likewise, it will be possible for a person to have become a general partner under Section 15904.01 without being designated as a general partner in the certificate of limited partnership. According to the last clause of this subdivision, the fact that a person is not listed as in the certificate as a general partner is not notice that the person is not a general partner. For further discussion of this point, see the Comment to Section 15904.01.

If the partnership agreement and the public record are inconsistent, Section 15902.01(d) applies (partnership agreement controls inter se; public record controls as to third parties who have relied). See also Section 15902.02(b) (requiring the limited partnership to amend its certificate of limited partnership to keep accurate the listing of general partners), 15902.02(c) (requiring a general partner to take corrective action when the general partner knows that the certificate of limited partnership contains false information), and 15902.08 (imposing liability for false information in inter alia the certificate of limited partnership).

**Subsection (d)**—This subdivision also provides what is commonly called constructive notice and works in conjunction with other sections of this chapter to curtail the power to bind and personal liability of general partners and persons dissociated as general partners. See Sections 15904.02, 15906.06, 15907.07, 15908.04, and 15908.05. Following RUPA (in substance, although not in form), the constructive notice begins 90 days after the effective date of the filed record. For the chapter's rules on delayed effective dates, see Section 15902.06(c).

The 90-day delay applies only to the constructive notice and not to the event described in the filed record.

Example: On March 15, X dissociates as a general partner from XYZ Limited Partnership by giving notice to XYZ. See Section 603(1). On March 20, XYZ amends its certificate of limited partnership to remove X's name from the list of general partners. See Section 15902.02(b)(2).

X's dissociation is effective March 15. If on March 16, X purports to be a general partner of XYZ and under Section 15906.06(a) binds XYZ to some obligation, X will be liable under Section 15906.06(b) as a "person dissociated as a general partner."

On June 13 (90 days after March 15), the world has constructive notice of X's dissociation as a general partner. Beginning on that date, X will lack the power to bind XYZ. See Section 15906.06(a)(2)(B) (person dissociated as a general partner can bind the limited partnership only if, inter alia, "at the time the other party enters into the transaction . . . the other party does not have notice of the dissociation").

Constructive notice under this subdivision applies to partners and transferees as well as other persons.

**Subsection (e)**—The phrase "person learns of it" in this subdivision is equivalent to the phrase "knows of it" in subdivision (b)(1).

**Subsection (h)**—Under this subdivision and Section 15903.02, information possessed by a person that is only a limited partner is not attributable to the limited partnership. However, information possessed by a person that is both a general partner and a limited partner is attributable to the limited partnership. See Section 15901.13 (Dual Capacity).

## SECTION 15901.04. NATURE, PURPOSE, AND DURATION OF ENTITY.

(a) A limited partnership is an entity distinct from its partners.

(b) A limited partnership may be organized under this chapter for any lawful purpose. A limited partnership may engage in any lawful business activity, whether or not for profit, except the banking business, the business of issuing policies of insurance and assuming insurance risks, or the trust company business.

(c) A limited partnership has a perpetual duration.

### Uniform Limited Partnership Act Comment

**Subsection (a)**—Acquiring or relinquishing an LLLP shield changes only the rules governing a general partner's liability for subsequently incurred obligations of the limited partnership. The underlying entity is unaffected.

**Subsection (b)**—In contrast with RULPA Section 106, this chapter does not require a limited partnership to have a business purpose. However, many of the chapter's default rules presuppose at least a profit-making purpose. See, e.g., Section 15905.03 (providing for the sharing of distributions in proportion to the value of contributions), 15907.01 (defining a transferable interest in terms of the right to receive distributions), 15908.01 (allocating the right to consent to cause or avoid dissolution in proportion to partners' rights to receive distributions), and 15908.09 (providing that, after a dissolved limited partnership has paid its creditors, "[a]ny surplus remaining . . . must be returned to the partners as they share in distributions"). If a limited partnership is organized for an essentially non-pecuniary purpose, the organizers should carefully review the chapter's default rules and override them as necessary via the partnership agreement.

**Subsection (c)**—The partnership agreement has the power to vary this subdivision, either by stating a definite term or by specifying an event or events which cause dissolution. Sections 15901.10(a) and 15908.01(1). Section 15908.01 also recognizes several other occurrences that cause dissolution. Thus, the public record pertaining to a limited partnership will not necessarily reveal whether the limited partnership actually has a perpetual duration.

The public record might also fail to reveal whether the limited partnership has in fact dissolved. A dissolved limited partnership may amend its certificate of limited partnership to indicate dissolution but is not required to do so. Section 15908.03(b)(1).

Predecessor law took a somewhat different approach. RULPA Section 201(4) required the certificate of limited partnership to state "the latest date upon which the limited partnership is to dissolve." Although RULPA Section 801(2) provided for a limited partnership to dissolve "upon the happening of events specified in writing in the partnership agreement," RULPA Section 203 required the limited partnership to file a certificate of cancellation to indicate that dissolution had occurred.

**SECTION 15901.05. POWERS.** A limited partnership has the powers to do all things necessary or convenient to carry on its activities, including the power to sue, be sued, and defend in its own name and to maintain an action against a partner for harm caused to the limited partnership by a breach of the partnership agreement or violation of a duty to the partnership.

## Uniform Limited Partnership Act Comment

This chapter omits as unnecessary any detailed list of specific powers. The power to sue and be sued is mentioned specifically so that Section 15901.10(b)(1) can prohibit the partnership agreement from varying that power. The power to maintain an action against a partner is mentioned specifically to establish that the limited partnership itself has standing to enforce the partnership agreement.

**SECTION 15901.06. GOVERNING LAW.** The law of this state governs relations among the partners of a limited partnership and between the partners and the limited partnership and the liability of partners as partners for an obligation of the limited partnership.

## Uniform Limited Partnership Act Comment

To partially define its scope, this section uses the phrase "relations among the partners of a limited partnership and between the partners and the limited partnership." Section 15901.10(a) uses essentially identical language in defining the proper realm of the partnership agreement: "relations among the partners and between the partners and the partnership."

Despite the similarity of language, this section has no bearing on the power of a partnership agreement to vary other provisions of this chapter. It is quite possible for a provision of this chapter to involve "relations among the partners of a limited partnership and between the partners and the limited partnership" and thus come within this section, and yet not be subject to variation by the partnership agreement. Although Section 15901.10(a) grants plenary authority to the partnership agreement to regulate "relations among the partners and between the partners and the partnership," that authority is subject to Section 15901.10(b).

For example, Section 15904.08 (General Standards of General Partners' Conduct) certainly involves "relations among the partners of a limited partnership and between the partners and the limited partnership." Therefore, according to this section, Section 15904.08 applies to a limited partnership formed or otherwise subject to this chapter. Just as certainly, Section 15904.08 pertains to "relations among the partners and between the partners and the partnership" for the purposes of Section 15901.10(a), and therefore the partnership agreement may properly address matters covered by Section 15904.08. However, Section 15901.10(b)(5), (6), and (7) limit the power of the partnership agreement to vary the rules stated in Section 15904.08. See also, e.g., Section 15905.02(c) (stating creditor's rights, which are protected under Section 15901.10(b)(13) from being restricted by the partnership agreement) and Comment to Section 15905.09.

This section also applies to "the liability of partners as partners for an obligation of a limited partnership." The phrase "as partners" contemplates the liability shield for limited partners under Section 15909.03. Other grounds for liability can be supplied by other law, including the law of some other jurisdiction. For example, a partner's contractual guaranty of a limited partnership obligation might well be governed by the law of some other jurisdiction.

Transferees derive their rights and status under this chapter from partners and accordingly this section applies to the relations of a transferee to the limited partnership.

The partnership agreement may not vary the rule stated in this section. See Section 15901.01(b)(2).

## SECTION 15901.07. SUPPLEMENTAL PRINCIPLES OF LAW; RATE OF INTEREST.

(a) Unless displaced by particular provisions of this chapter, the principles of law and equity supplement this chapter.

(b) If an obligation to pay interest arises under this chapter and the rate is not specified, the rate is that specified in Section 3289 of the Civil Code.

## Uniform Limited Partnership Act Comment

**Subsection (a)**—This language comes from RUPA Section 104 and does not address an important question raised by the de-linking of this chapter from the UPA and RUPA—namely, to what extent is the case law of general partnerships relevant to limited partnerships governed by this chapter?

Predecessor law, RULPA Section 403, expressly equated the rights, powers, restrictions, and liabilities of a general partner in a limited partnership with the rights, powers, restrictions, and liabilities of a partner in a general partnership. This chapter has no comparable provision. Therefore, a court should not assume that a case concerning a general partnership is automatically relevant to a limited partnership governed by this chapter. A general partnership case may be relevant by analogy, especially if (1) the issue in dispute involves a provision of this chapter for which a comparable provision exists under the law of general partnerships; and (2) the fundamental differences between a general partnership and limited partnership are immaterial to the disputed issue.

## SECTION 15901.08. NAME.

(a) The name of a limited partnership may contain the name of any partner.

(b) The name of a limited partnership must contain the phrase "limited partnership" or the abbreviation "L.P." or "LP" at the end of its name.

(c) The name of a foreign limited liability limited partnership that is applying for a certificate of registration pursuant to Section 15909.02 must contain the phrase "limited liability limited partnership" or the abbreviation "LLLP" or "L.L.L.P." and must not contain the abbreviation "L.P." or "LP."

(d) Unless authorized by subdivision (e), the name of a limited partnership must be distinguishable in the records of the Secretary of State from:

(1) the name of any limited partnership that has previously filed a certificate pursuant to Section 15902.01 or any foreign limited partnership registered pursuant to Section 15909.01; and (2) each name reserved under Section 15901.09.

(e) A limited partnership may apply to the Secretary of State for authorization to use a name that does not comply with subdivision (d). The Secretary of State shall authorize use of the name applied for if, as to each conflicting name:

(1) the present user, registrant, or owner of the conflicting name consents in a signed record to the use and submits an undertaking in a form satisfactory to the Secretary of State to change the conflicting name to a name that complies with subdivision (d) and is distin-

guishable in the records of the Secretary of State from the name applied for;

(2) the applicant delivers to the Secretary of State a certified copy of the final judgment of a court of competent jurisdiction establishing the applicant's right to use in this state the name applied for; or

(3) the applicant delivers to the Secretary of State proof satisfactory to the Secretary of State that the present user, registrant, or owner of the conflicting name:

(A) has merged into the applicant;

(B) has been converted into the applicant; or

(C) has transferred substantially all of its assets, including the conflicting name, to the applicant.

(f) Subject to Section 15909.05, this section applies to any foreign limited partnership transacting business in this state, having a certificate of registration to transact business in this state, or applying for a certificate of registration.

(g) The name of a limited partnership may not contain the words "bank," "insurance," "trust," "trustee," "incorporated," "inc.," "corporation," or "corp."

## Uniform Limited Partnership Act Comment

**Subsection (a)**—Predecessor law, RULPA Section 102, prohibited the use of a limited partner's name in the name of a limited partnership except in unusual circumstances. That approach derived from the 1916 Uniform Limited Partnership chapter and has become antiquated. In 1916, most business organizations were either unshielded (e.g., general partnerships) or partially shielded (*e.g.*, limited partnerships), and it was reasonable for third parties to believe that an individual whose own name appeared in the name of a business would "stand behind" the business. Today most businesses have a full shield (e.g., corporations, limited liability companies, most limited liability partnerships), and corporate, LLC and LLP statutes generally pose no barrier to the use of an owner's name in the name of the entity. This chapter eliminates RULPA's restriction and puts limited partnerships on equal footing with these other "shielded" entities.

**Subsection (d)(1)**—If a sole proprietor registers or reserves a business name under a fictitious name statute, that name comes within this provision. For the purposes of this provision, a sole proprietor doing business under a registered or reserved name is a "person other than an individual."

**Subsection (f)**—Section 15909.05 permits a foreign limited partnership to obtain a certificate of authority under an alternate name if the foreign limited partnership's actual name does not comply with this section.

## SECTION 15901.09. RESERVATION OF NAME.

(a) The exclusive right to the use of a name that complies with Section 15901.08 may be reserved by:

(1) a person intending to organize a limited partnership under this chapter and to adopt the name;

(2) a limited partnership or a foreign limited partnership authorized to transact business in this state intending to adopt the name;

(3) a foreign limited partnership intending to obtain a certificate of registration to transact business in this state and adopt the name;

(4) a person intending to organize a foreign limited partnership and intending to have it obtain a certificate of registration to transact business in this state and adopt the name;

(5) a foreign limited partnership formed under the name; or

(6) a foreign limited partnership formed under a name that does not comply with subdivision (b) or (c) of Section 15901.08, but the name reserved under this paragraph may differ from the foreign limited partnership's name only to the extent necessary to comply with subdivision (b) or (c) of Section 15901.08.

(b) A person may apply to reserve a name under subdivision (a) by delivering to the Secretary of State an application that states the name to be reserved and the paragraph of subdivision (a) which applies. If the Secretary of State finds that the name is available for use by the applicant, the Secretary of State shall issue a certificate of name reservation and thereby reserve the name for the exclusive use of the applicant for 60 days.

(c) An applicant that has reserved a name pursuant to subdivision (b) may reserve the same name for an additional 60-day period. The Secretary of State shall not issue a certificate reserving the same name for two or more consecutive 60-day periods to the same applicant or for the use or benefit of the same person.

(d) A person that has reserved a name under this section may transfer the reserved name to another person, effective upon delivery to the Secretary of State of a notice of transfer that states the reserved name, the name and address of the person to which the reservation is to be transferred, and the paragraph of subdivision (a) which applies to the other person.

**SECTION 15901.10. EFFECT OF PARTNERSHIP AGREE-MENT; NONWAIVABLE PROVISIONS.**

(a) Except as otherwise provided in subdivision (b), the partnership agreement governs relations among the partners and between the partners and the partnership. To the extent the partnership agreement does not otherwise provide, this chapter governs relations among the partners and between the partners and the partnership.

(b) A partnership agreement may not:

(1) vary a limited partnership's power under Section 15901.05 to sue, be sued, and defend in its own name;

(2) vary the law applicable to a limited partnership under Section 15901.06;

(3) vary the requirements of Section 15902.04;

(4) vary the information required under Section 15901.11 or unreasonably restrict the right to information under Section 15903.04 or 15904.07, but the partnership agreement may impose reasonable restrictions on the availability and use of information obtained under those sections and may define appropriate remedies, including liquidated damages, for a breach of any reasonable restriction on use;

(5) eliminate the duty of loyalty under Section 15904.08, but the partnership agreement may:

(A) identify specific types or categories of activities that do not violate the duty of loyalty, if not manifestly unreasonable; and

(B) specify the number or percentage of partners which may authorize or ratify, after full disclosure to all partners of all material facts, a specific act or transaction that otherwise would violate the duty of loyalty;

(6) unreasonably reduce the duty of care under subdivision (c) of Section 15904.08;

(7) eliminate the obligation of good faith and fair dealing under subdivision (b) of Section 15903.05 and subdivision (d) of Section 15904.08, but the partnership agreement may prescribe the standards by which the performance of the obligation is to be measured, if the standards are not manifestly unreasonable;

(8) vary the power of a person to dissociate as a general partner under subdivision (a) of Section 15906.04 except to require that the notice under subdivision (a) of Section 15906.03 be in a record;

(9) eliminate the power of a court to decree dissolution in the circumstances specified in subdivision (a) of Section 15908.02;

(10) vary the requirement to wind up the partnership's business as specified in Section 15908.03;

(11) unreasonably restrict the right to maintain an action under Article 10 (commencing with Section 15910.01);

(12) restrict the right of a partner to approve a conversion or merger;

(13) vary the provisions of Article 11.5 (commencing with Section 15911.14), except to the extent expressly permitted by such provisions; or

(14) restrict rights under this chapter of a person other than a partner or a transferee.

## Uniform Limited Partnership Act Comment

**Source**—RUPA Section 103.

Subject only to subdivision (b), the partnership agreement has plenary power to structure and regulate the relations of the partners inter se. Although the certificate of limited partnership is a limited partnership's foundational document, among the partners the partnership agreement controls. See Section 15902.01(d).

The partnership agreement has the power to control the manner of its own amendment. In particular, a provision of the agreement prohibiting oral modifications is enforceable, despite any common law antagonism to "no oral modification" provisions. Likewise, a partnership agreement can impose "made in a record" requirements on other aspects of the partners' relationship, such as requiring consents to be made in a record and signed, or rendering unenforceable oral promises to make contributions or oral understandings as to "events upon the happening of which the limited partnership is to be dissolved," Section 15901.11(8)(D). See also Section 15908.01(1).

**Subsection (b)(3)**—The referenced section states who must sign various documents.

**Subsection (b)(4)**—In determining whether a restriction is reasonable, a court might consider: (i) the danger or other problem the restriction seeks to avoid; (ii) the purpose for which the information is sought; and (iii) whether, in light of both the problem and the purpose, the restriction is reasonably tailored. Restricting access to or use of the names and addresses of limited partners is not per se unreasonable.

Under this chapter, general and limited partners have sharply different roles. A restriction that is reasonable as to a limited partner is not necessarily reasonable as to a general partner.

Sections 15903.04(g) and 15904.07(f) authorize the limited partnership (as distinguished from the partnership agreement) to impose restrictions on the use of information. For a comparison of restrictions contained in the partnership agreement and restrictions imposed unilaterally by the limited partnership, see the Comment to Section 15903.04(g).

**Subsection (b)(5)(A)**—It is not per se manifestly unreasonable for the partnership agreement to permit a general partner to compete with the limited partnership.

**Subsection (b)(5)(B)**—The chapter does not require that the authorization or ratification be by disinterested partners, although the partnership agreement may so provide. The chapter does require that the disclosure be made to all partners, even if the partnership agreement excludes some partners from the authorization or ratification process. An interested partner that participates in the authorization or ratification process is subject to the obligation of good faith and fair dealing. Sections 15903.05(b) and 15904.08(d).

**Subsection (b)(8)**—This restriction applies only to the power of a person to dissociate as a general partner. The partnership agreement may eliminate the power of a person to dissociate as a limited partner.

**Subsection (b)(9)**—This provision should not be read to limit a partnership agreement's power to provide for arbitration. For example, an agreement to arbitrate all disputes—including dissolution disputes—is enforceable. Any other interpretation would put this chapter at odds with federal law. See *Southland Corp. v Keating* (1984) 465 US 1 (holding that the Federal Arbitration chapter preempts state statutes that seek to invalidate agreements to arbitrate) and *Allied-Bruce Terminix Cos., Inc. v Dobson* (1995) 513 US 265 (same). This provision does prohibit any narrowing of the substantive grounds for judicial dissolution as stated in Section 15908.02.

Example: A provision of a partnership agreement states that no partner may obtain judicial dissolution without showing that a general partner is in material breach of the partnership agreement. The provision is ineffective to prevent a court from ordering dissolution under Section 15908.02.

**Subsection (b)(11)**—Section 15910.01 codifies a partner's right to bring a direct action, and the rest of Article 10 provides for derivative actions. The partnership agreement may not restrict a partner's right to bring either type of action if the effect is to undercut or frustrate the duties and rights protected by Section 15901.01(b).

The reasonableness of a restriction on derivative actions should be judged in light of the history and purpose of derivative actions. They originated as an equitable remedy, intended to protect passive owners against management abuses. A partnership agreement may not provide that all derivative claims will be subject to final determination by a special litigation committee appointed by the limited partnership, because that provision would eliminate, not merely restrict, a partner's right to bring a derivative action.

**Subsection (b)(12)**—Section 15911.10 imposes special consent requirements with regard to transactions that might make a partner personally liable for entity debts.

**Subsection (b)(13)**—The partnership agreement is a contract, and this provision reflects a basic notion of contract law—namely, that a contract can directly restrict rights only of parties to the contract and of persons who derive their rights from the contract. A provision of a partnership agreement can be determined to be unenforceable against third parties under paragraph (b)(13) without therefore and automatically being unenforceable inter se the partners and any transferees. How the former determination affects the latter question is a matter of other law.

## SECTION 15901.11. REQUIRED INFORMATION. A limited partnership shall maintain at its designated office the following information:

(1) a current list showing the full name and last known street and mailing address of each partner, separately identifying the general partners, in alphabetical order, and the limited partners, in alphabetical order;

(2) a copy of the initial certificate of limited partnership and all amendments to and restatements of the certificate, together with signed copies of any powers of attorney under which any certificate, amendment, or restatement has been signed;

(3) a copy of any filed certificate of conversion or merger;

(4) a copy of the limited partnership's federal, state, and local income tax returns and reports, if any, for the six most recent years;

(5) a copy of any partnership agreement made in a record and any amendment made in a record to any partnership agreement;

(6) a copy of any financial statement of the limited partnership for the six most recent years;

(7) a copy of any record made by the limited partnership during the past three years of any consent given by or vote taken of any partner pursuant to this chapter or the partnership agreement; and

(8) unless contained in a partnership agreement made in a record, a record stating:

(A) the amount of cash, and a description and statement of the agreed value of the other benefits, contributed and agreed to be contributed by each partner;

(B) (1) the times at which, or events on the happening of which, any additional contributions agreed to be made by each partner are to be made;

(C) for any person that is both a general partner and a limited partner, a specification of what transferable interest the person owns in each capacity; and

(D) any events upon the happening of which the limited partnership is to be dissolved and its activities wound up.

## Uniform Limited Partnership Act Comment

**Source**—RULPA Section 105. Sections 15903.04 and 15904.07 govern access to the information required by this section, as well as to other information pertaining to a limited partnership.

**Paragraph (5)**—This requirement applies to superseded as well as current agreements and amendments. An agreement or amendment is "made in a record " to the extent the agreement is "integrated" into a record and consented to in that memorialized form. It is possible for a partnership agreement to be made in part in a record and in part otherwise. See Comment to Section 15901.10. An oral agreement that is subsequently inscribed in a record (but not consented to as such) was not "made in a record" and is not covered by paragraph (5). However, if the limited partnership happens to have such a record, Section 15903.04(b) might and Section 15904.07(a)(2) will provide a right of access.

**Paragraph (7)**—This paragraph does not require a limited partnership to make a record of consents given and votes taken. However, if the limited partnership has made such a record, this paragraph requires that the limited partnership maintain the record for three years. The requirement applies to any record made by the limited partnership, not just to records made contemporaneously with the giving of consent or voting. The three-year period runs from when the record was made and not from when the consent was given or vote taken.

**Paragraph (8)**—Information is "contained in a partnership agreement made in a record" only to the extent that the information is "integrated" into a record and, in that memorialized form, has been consented to as part of the partnership agreement.

This paragraph is not a statute of frauds provision. For example, failure to comply with paragraph (8)(A) or (B) does not render unenforceable an oral promise to make a contribution. Likewise, failure to comply with paragraph (8)(D) does not invalidate an oral term of the partnership specifying "events upon the happening of which the limited partnership is to be dissolved and its activities wound up." See also Section 15908.01(a).

Obversely, the mere fact that a limited partnership maintains a record in purported compliance with paragraph (8)(A) or (B) does not prove that a person has actually promised to make a contribution. Likewise, the mere fact that a limited partnership maintains a record in purported compliance with paragraph (8)(D) does not prove that the partnership agreement actually includes the specified events as causes of dissolution.

Consistent with the partnership agreement's plenary power to structure and regulate the relations of the partners inter se, a partnership agreement can impose "made in a record" requirements which render unenforceable oral promises to make contributions or oral understandings as to "events upon the happening of which the limited partnership is to be dissolved." See Comment to Section 15901.10.

**Paragraph (8)(A) and (B)**—Often the partnership agreement will state in record form the value of contributions made and promised to be made. If not, these provisions require that the value be stated in a record maintained as part of the limited partnership's required information. The chapter does not authorize the limited partnership or the general partners to set the value of a contribution without the concurrence of the person who has made or promised the contribution, although the partnership agreement itself can grant that authority.

**Paragraph (8)(C)**—The information required by this provision is essential for determining what happens to the transferable interests of a person that is both a general partner and a limited partner and that dissociates in one of those capacities but not the other. See Sections 15906.02(9) and 15906.05(a).

## SECTION 15901.12. BUSINESS TRANSACTIONS OF PARTNER WITH PARTNERSHIP.

A partner may lend money to and transact other business with the limited partnership and has the same rights and obligations with respect to the loan or other transaction as a person that is not a partner.

## Uniform Limited Partnership Act Comment

**Source**—RULPA Section 107. See also RUPA Section 404(f) and ULLCA Section 409(f).

This section has no impact on a general partner's duty under Section 15904.08(b)(2) (duty of loyalty includes refraining from acting as or for an adverse party) and means rather that this chapter does not discriminate against a creditor of a limited partnership that happens also to be a partner. See, *e.g., BTI v Equitable Life Assurance Society of the United States* (CA 4 Dist.1999) 75 CA4th 1406, 1415, 89 CR2d 811, 814 and *SEC v DuPont, Homsey & Co.* (D. Mass 1962 204 F Supp 944, 946), vacated and remanded on other grounds, 334 F2d 704 (1st Cir 1964). This section does not, however, override other law, such as fraudulent transfer or conveyance acts.

**SECTION 15901.13. DUAL CAPACITY.** A person may be both a general partner and a limited partner. A person that is both a general and limited partner has the rights, powers, duties, and obligations provided by this chapter and the partnership agreement in each of those capacities. When the person acts as a general partner, the person is subject to the obligations, duties and restrictions under this chapter and the partnership agreement for general partners. When the person acts as a limited partner, the person is subject to the obligations, duties and restrictions under this chapter and the partnership agreement for limited partners.

## Uniform Limited Partnership Act Comment

**Source**—RULPA Section 404, redrafted for reasons of style.

**SECTION 15901.14. OFFICE AND AGENT FOR SERVICE OF PROCESS.**

(a) A limited partnership shall designate and continuously maintain in this state:

(1) an office, which need not be a place of its activity in this state; and

(2) an agent for service of process.

(b) A foreign limited partnership shall designate and continuously maintain in this state an agent for service of process.

(c) An agent for service of process of a limited partnership or foreign limited partnership must be an individual who is a resident of this state or a corporation that has complied with Section 1505 of the Corporations Code and whose capacity to act as an agent has not terminated.

## Uniform Limited Partnership Act Comment

**Subsection (a)**—The initial designation occurs in the original certificate of limited partnership. Section 15902.01(a)(2). A limited partnership may change the designation by a certificate of amendment, Section 15902.02. If a limited partnership fails to maintain an agent for service of process, substituted service may be made on the Secretary of State. Section 15901.16(b).

**Subsection (b)**—The initial designation occurs in the application for a certificate of authority. See Section 15909.02(a)(4). A foreign limited partnership may change the designation by a certificate of amendment. If a foreign limited partnership fails to maintain an agent for service of process, substituted service may be made on the Secretary of State. Section 15901.16(b). A foreign limited partnership's failure to maintain an agent for service of process is grounds for administrative revocation of the certificate of authority.

A foreign limited partnership need not maintain an office in this State.

## SECTION 15901.15. CONSENT AND PROXIES OF PARTNERS. Action requiring the consent of partners under this chapter may be taken without a meeting, and a partner may appoint a proxy to consent or otherwise act for the partner by signing an appointment record, either personally or by the partner's attorney in fact.

## Uniform Limited Partnership Act Comment

**Source**—ULLCA Section 404(d and (e).

This chapter imposes no meeting requirement and does not distinguish among oral, record, express and tacit consent. The partnership agreement may establish such requirements and make such distinctions.

## SECTION 15901.16. SERVICE OF PROCESS; PRODUCTION OF BOOKS AND RECORDS.

(a) In addition to Chapter 4 (commencing with Section 413.10) of Title 5 of Part 2 of the Code of Civil Procedure, process may be served upon limited partnerships and foreign limited partnerships as provided in this section.

(b) Personal service of a copy of any process against the limited partnership or the foreign limited partnership will constitute valid service on the limited partnership if delivered either: (1) to any individual designated by it as agent or, if a limited partnership, to any general partner or (2) if the designated agent or, if a limited partnership, general partner is a corporation, to any person named in the latest certificate of the corporate agent filed pursuant to Section 1505 of the Corporations Code at the office of the corporate agent or to any officer of the general partner, shall constitute valid service on the limited partnership or the foreign limited partnership. No change in the address of the agent for service of process where the agent is an individual or appointment of a new agent for service of process shall be effective (1) for a limited partnership until an amendment to the certificate of limited partnership is filed or (2) for a foreign limited partnership until an amendment to the application for registration is filed. In the case of a foreign limited partnership that has appointed the Secretary of State as agent for service of process by reason of subdivision (e) of Section 15909.07, process shall be delivered by hand to the Secretary of State, or to any person employed in the capacity of assistant or deputy, which shall be one copy of the process for each defendant to be served, together with a copy of the court order authorizing the service and the fee therefor. The order shall include and set forth an address to which such process shall be sent by the Secretary of State.

(c) (1) If an agent for service of process has resigned and has not been replaced or if the agent designated cannot with reasonable diligence be found at the address designated for personal delivery of the process, and it is shown by affidavit to the satisfaction of the court that process against a limited partnership or foreign limited partnership cannot be served with reasonable diligence upon the designated agent or, if a foreign limited partnership, upon any general partner by hand in the manner provided in Section 415.10, subdivision (a) of Section 415.20 or subdivision (a) of Section 415.30, of the Code of Civil Procedure, the court may make an order that the service shall be made upon a domestic limited partnership which has filed a certificate or upon a foreign limited partnership which has a certificate of registration to transact business in this state by delivering by hand to the Secretary of State, or to any person employed in the Secretary of State's office in the capacity of assistant or deputy, one copy of the process for each defendant to be served, together with a copy of the order authorizing the service. Service in this manner shall be deemed complete on the 10th day after delivery of the process to the Secretary of State.

(2) Upon receipt of any such copy of process and the fee therefor, the Secretary of State shall give notice of the service of the process to the limited partnership or foreign limited partnership, at its principal office, by forwarding to that office, by registered mail with request for return receipt the copy of the process.

(3) The Secretary of State shall keep a record of all process served upon the Secretary of State under this chapter and shall record therein

the time of service and the Secretary of State's action with reference thereto. A certificate under the Secretary of State's official seal, certifying to the receipt of process, the giving of notice thereof to the limited partnership or foreign limited partnership, and the forwarding of the process pursuant to this section, shall be competent and prima facie evidence of the matters stated therein.

(d) (1) The certificate of a limited partnership and the application for a certificate of registration of a foreign limited partnership shall designate, as the agent for service of process, an individual residing in this state or a corporation which has complied with Section 1505 of the Corporations Code and whose capacity to act as an agent has not terminated. If an individual is designated, the statement shall set forth that person's complete business or residence address in this state. If a corporate agent is designated, no address for it shall be set forth.

(2) An agent designated for service of process may file with the Secretary of State a signed and acknowledged written statement of resignation as an agent. Thereupon the authority of the agent to act in that capacity shall cease and the Secretary of State forthwith shall give written notice of the filing of the certificate of resignation by mail to the limited partnership or foreign limited partnership addressed to its designated office.

(3) If an individual who has been designated agent for service of process dies or resigns or no longer resides in the state or if the corporate agent for that purpose, resigns, dissolves, withdraws from the state, forfeits its right to transact intrastate business, has its corporate rights, powers and privileges suspended or ceases to exist, (A) the limited partnership shall promptly file an amendment to the certificate designating a new agent or (B) the foreign limited partnership shall promptly file an amendment to the application for registration.

(e) In addition to any other discovery rights which may exist, in any case pending in a California court having jurisdiction in which a party seeks records from a partnership formed under this chapter, whether or not the partnership is a party, the court shall have the power to order the production in California of the books and records of the partnership on the terms and conditions that the court deems appropriate.

## California Code Comment
### By Phil Jelsma

Source—California Corporations Code Section 15627.

## SECTION 15901.17. JURISDICTION; ARBITRATION; SERVICE OF PROCESS; CONSENT.

(a) A partner may, in a written partnership agreement or other writing, consent to be subject to the nonexclusive jurisdiction of the courts of a specified jurisdiction, or the exclusive jurisdiction of the courts of this state.

(b) If a partner desires to use the arbitration process, that partner may in a written partnership agreement or other writing, consent to be nonexclusively subject to arbitration in a specified state, or to be exclusively subject to arbitration in this state.

(c) Along with this consent to the jurisdiction of courts or arbitration, a partner may consent to be served with legal process in the manner prescribed in the partnership agreement or other writing.

## California Code Comment
### By Phil Jelsma

Source—California Corporations Code Section 15627.5.

## ARTICLE 2.
## FORMATION; CERTIFICATE OF
## LIMITED PARTNERSHIP AND OTHER FILINGS

## SECTION 15902.01. FORMATION OF LIMITED PARTNERSHIP; CERTIFICATE OF LIMITED PARTNERSHIP.

(a) In order for a limited partnership to be formed, a certificate of limited partnership must be filed with and on a form prescribed by the Secretary of State and, either before or after the filing of a certificate of limited partnership, the partners shall have entered into a partnership agreement. The certificate must state:

(1) the name of the limited partnership, which must comply with Section 15901.08;

(2) the address of the initial designated office;

(3) the name and address of the initial agent for service of process in accordance with paragraph (1) of subdivision (a) of Section 15901.16; and

(4) the name and the address of each general partner.

(b) A certificate of limited partnership may also contain any other matters but may not vary or otherwise affect the provisions specified in subdivision (b) of Section 15901.10 in a manner inconsistent with that section.

(c) Subject to subdivision (c) of Section 15902.06 a limited partnership is formed when the Secretary of State files the certificate of limited partnership.

(d) Subject to subdivision (b), if any provision of a partnership agreement is inconsistent with the filed certificate of limited partnership or with a filed certificate of dissociation, cancellation, or amendment or filed certificate of conversion or merger:

(1) the partnership agreement prevails as to partners and transferees; and

(2) the filed certificate of limited partnership, certificate of dissociation, cancellation, or amendment or filed certificate of conversion or merger prevails as to persons, other than partners and transferees, that reasonably rely on the filed record to their detriment.

(e) A limited partnership may record in the office of the county recorder of any county in this state a certified copy of the certificate of limited partnership, or any amendment thereto, which has been filed by the Secretary of State. A foreign limited partnership may record in the office of the county recorder of any county in the state a certified copy of the application for registration to transact business, together with the certificate of registration, referred to in Section 15909.02, or any amendment thereto, which has been filed by the Secretary of State. The recording shall create a conclusive presumption in favor of any bona fide purchaser or encumbrancer for value of the partnership real property located in the county in which the certified copy has been recorded, that the persons named as general partners therein are the general partners of the partnership named and that they are all of the general partners of the partnership.

(f) The Secretary of State may cancel the filing of certificates of limited partnership if a check or other remittance accepted in payment of the filing fee is not paid upon presentation. For partners and transferees, the partnership agreement is paramount. Upon receiving written notification that the item presented for payment has not been honored for payment, the Secretary of State shall give a first written notice of the applicability of this section to the agent for service of process or to the person submitting the instrument. Thereafter, if the amount has not been paid by cashier's check or equivalent, the Secretary of State shall give a second written notice of cancellation and the cancellation shall thereupon be effective. The second notice shall be given 20 days or more after the first notice and 90 days or less after the original filing.

(g) The Secretary of State shall include with instructional materials, provided in conjunction with the form for filing a certificate of limited partnership under subdivision (a), a notice that the filing of the certificate of limited partnership will obligate the limited partnership to pay an annual tax for that taxable year to the Franchise Tax Board pursuant to Section 17935 of the Revenue and Taxation Code. That notice shall be updated annually to specify the dollar amount of the annual tax.

## Uniform Limited Partnership Act Comment

**Source**—RULPA Section 201.

A limited partnership is a creature of statute, and this section governs how a limited partnership comes into existence. A limited partnership is formed only if (i) a certificate of limited partnership is prepared and delivered to the specified public official for filing, (ii) the public official files the certificate, and (iii) the certificate, delivery and filing are in "substantial compliance" with the requirements of subdivision (a). Section 15902.06(c) governs when a limited partnership comes into existence.

Despite its foundational importance, a certificate of limited partnership is far less powerful than a corporation's articles of incorporation. Among partners and transferees, for example, the partnership agreement is paramount. See Section 15902.01(d).

**Subsection (a)(1)** -Section 15901.08 contains name requirements. To be acceptable for filing, a certificate of limited partnership must state a name for the limited partnership which complies with Section 15901.08.

**Subsection (a)(3)**—This provision should be read in conjunction with Section 15901.03(c) and Section 15904.01 and the Comment to those sections.

**Subsection (d)**—Source: ULLCA Section 203(c).

A limited partnership is a creature of contract as well as a creature of statute. It will be possible, albeit improper, for the partnership agreement to be inconsistent with the certificate of limited partnership or other specified public filings relating to the limited partnership. For those circumstances, this subdivision provides the rule for determining which source of information prevails.

For partners and transferees, the partnership agreement is paramount. For third parties seeking to invoke the public record, actual knowledge of that record is necessary and notice under Section 15901.03(c) or (d) is irrelevant. A third party wishing to enforce the public record over the partnership agreement must show reasonable reliance on the public record and reliance presupposes knowledge.

This subdivision does not expressly cover a situation in which (i) one of the specified filed records contains information in addition to, but not inconsistent with, the partnership agreement, and (ii) a person, other than a partner or transferee, detrimentally relies on the additional information. However, the policy reflected in this subdivision seems equally applicable to that situation.

Responsibility for maintaining a limited partnership's public record rests with the general partner or partners. Section 15902.02(c). A general partner's failure to meet that responsibility can expose the general partner to liability to third parties under Section 15902.08(a)(2) and might constitute a breach of the general partner's duties under Section 15904.08. In addition, an aggrieved person may seek a remedy under Section 15902.05 (Signing and Filing Pursuant to Judicial Order).

## SECTION 15902.02. AMENDMENT OR RESTATEMENT OF CERTIFICATE.

(a) In order to amend its certificate of limited partnership, a limited partnership must deliver to and on a form prescribed by the Secretary of State for filing an amendment stating:

(1) the name and the Secretary of State's file number of the limited partnership; and

(2) the changes the amendment makes to the certificate as most recently amended or restated.

(b) A limited partnership shall promptly deliver to the Secretary of State for filing an amendment to a certificate of limited partnership to reflect:

(1) the admission of a new general partner;

(2) the dissociation of a person as a general partner; or

(3) the appointment of a person to wind up the limited partnership's activities under subdivisions (c) or (d) of Section 15908.03.

(c) A general partner that knows that any information in a filed certificate of limited partnership was false when the certificate was filed or has become false due to changed circumstances shall promptly:

(1) cause the certificate to be amended; or

(2) if appropriate, deliver to the Secretary of State for filing an amendment or a certificate of correction pursuant to Section 15902.07.

(d) A certificate of limited partnership may be amended at any time for any other proper purpose as determined by the limited partnership.

(e) A restated certificate of limited partnership may be delivered to and on a form prescribed by the Secretary of State for filing in the same manner as an amendment.

(1) A restated certificate of limited partnership may be filed that embodies all of the provisions that are in effect contained in the different certificates that have been filed with the Secretary of State.

(2) A restated certificate of limited partnership may include an amendment of the certificate of limited partnership not previously filed with the Secretary of State.

(3) The restated certificate of limited partnership shall supersede the initial certificate of limited partnership and all amendments thereto previously filed with the Secretary of State.

(4) Any amendment effected in connection with the restatement of the certificate of limited partnership shall be subject to any other provision of this chapter not inconsistent with this section that would apply if a separate certificate of amendment were filed to effect that amendment.

(f) Subject to subdivision (c) of Section 15902.06, an amendment or restated certificate is effective when filed by the Secretary of State.

### Uniform Limited Partnership Act Comment

**Source**—RULPA Section 202.

**Subsection (b)**—This subdivision lists changes in circumstances which require an amendment to the certificate.

This subdivision states an obligation of the limited partnership. However, so long as the limited partnership has at least one general partner, the general partner or partners are responsible for managing the limited partnership's activities. Section 15904.06(a). That management responsibility includes maintaining accuracy in the limited partnership's public record. Moreover, subdivision (c) imposes direct responsibility on any general partner that knows that the filed certificate of limited partnership contains false information.

**Subsection (c)**—This provision imposes an obligation directly on the general partners rather than on the limited partnership. A general partner's failure to meet that responsibility can expose the general partner to liability to third parties under Section 15902.08(a)(2) and might constitute a breach of the general partner's duties under Section 15904.08. In addition, an aggrieved person may seek a remedy under Section 15902.05 (Signing and Filing Pursuant to Judicial Order).

**Subsection (d)**—A limited partnership that desires to change its name will have to amend its certificate of limited partnership. The new name will have to comply with Section 15901.08. See Section 15902.01(a)(1).

## SECTION 15902.03. CERTIFICATE OF CANCELLATION.

A dissolved limited partnership that has completed winding up shall deliver to and on a form prescribed by the Secretary of State for filing a certificate of cancellation that states:

(1) the name of the limited partnership and the Secretary of State's file number;

(2) the date of filing of its initial certificate of limited partnership; and

(3) any other information as determined by the general partners filing the certificate or by a person appointed pursuant to subdivisions (c) or (d) of Section 15908.03.

### Uniform Limited Partnership Act Comment

Under Section 15901.03(d)(3), a filed certificate of cancellation provides constructive notice, 90 days after the statement's effective date, that the limited partnership is terminated. That notice effectively terminates any apparent authority to bind the limited partnership.

However, this section is permissive. Therefore, it is not possible to use Section 15902.05 (Signing and Filing Pursuant to Judicial Order) to cause a certificate of cancellation to be filed.

### SECTION 15902.04. SIGNING OF RECORDS.

(a) Each record delivered to the Secretary of State for filing pursuant to this chapter must be signed in the following manner:

(1) An initial certificate of limited partnership must be signed by all general partners listed in the certificate.

(2) An amendment designating as general partner a person admitted under paragraph (2) of subdivision (c) of Section 15908.01 following the dissociation of a limited partnership's last general partner must be signed by that person.

(3) An amendment required by subdivision (c) of Section 15908.03 following the appointment of a person to wind up the dissolved limited partnership's activities must be signed by that person.

(4) Any other amendment must be signed by:

(A) at least one general partner listed in the certificate of limited partnership;

(B) each other person designated in the amendment as a new general partner; and

(C) each person that the amendment indicates has dissociated as a general partner, unless:

(i) the person is deceased or a guardian or general conservator has been appointed for the person and the amendment so states; or

(ii) the person has previously delivered to the Secretary of State for filing a certificate of dissociation.

(5) A restated certificate of limited partnership must be signed by at least one general partner listed in the certificate, and, to the extent the restated certificate effects a change under any other para-

graph of this subdivision, the restated certificate must be signed in a manner that satisfies that paragraph.

(6) A certificate of cancellation must be signed by all general partners listed in the certificate of limited partnership or, if the certificate of limited partnership of a dissolved limited partnership lists no general partners, by the person appointed pursuant to subdivisions (c) or (d) of Section 15908.03 to wind up the dissolved limited partnership's activities.

(7) Certificates of conversion must be signed as provided in subdivision (b) of Section 15911.06.

(8) Certificates of merger must be signed as provided in subdivision (a) of Section 15911.14.

(9) Any other record delivered on behalf of a limited partnership to the Secretary of State for filing must be signed by at least one general partner listed in the certificate of limited partnership.

(10) A certificate of dissociation by a person pursuant to paragraph (4) of subdivision (a) of Section 15906.05 stating that the person has dissociated as a general partner must be signed by that person.

(11) A certificate of withdrawal by a person pursuant to Section 15903.06 must be signed by that person.

(12) A record delivered on behalf of a foreign limited partnership to the Secretary of State for filing must be signed by at least one general partner of the foreign limited partnership.

(13) Any other record delivered on behalf of any person to the Secretary of State for filing must be signed by that person.

(b) Any person may sign by an attorney in fact any record to be filed pursuant to this chapter.

(c) The Secretary of State shall not be required to verify that the person withdrawing or dissociating was ever actually named in an official filing as a general or limited partner.

## Uniform Limited Partnership Act Comment

**Source**—ULLCA Section 205.

This section pertains only to signing requirements and implies nothing about approval requirements.

A person who signs a record without ascertaining that the record has been properly authorized risks liability under Section 15902.08.

**Subsection (a)**—The recurring reference to general partners "listed in the certificate" recognizes that a person might be admitted as a general partner under Section 15904.01 without immediately being listed in the certificate of limited partnership. Such persons may have rights, powers and obligations despite their unlisted status, but they cannot act as general partners for the purpose of affecting the limited partnership's public record. See the Comment to Section 15901.03(c) and the Comment to Section 15904.01.

## SECTION 15902.05. SIGNING AND FILING PURSUANT TO JUDICIAL ORDER.

(a) If a person required by this chapter to sign a record or deliver a record to the Secretary of State for filing does not do so, any other person that is aggrieved may petition the superior court to order:

(1) the person to sign the record;

(2) deliver the record to the Secretary of State for filing; or

(3) the Secretary of State to file the record unsigned.

(b) If the person aggrieved under subdivision (a) is not the limited partnership or foreign limited partnership to which the record pertains, the aggrieved person shall make the limited partnership or foreign limited partnership a party to the action. A person aggrieved under subdivision (a) may seek the remedies provided in subdivision (a) in the same action in combination or in the alternative. In any action under this subdivision, if the court finds the failure of the person to comply with the requirement to sign a record or deliver a record to the Secretary of State for filing to have been without justification, the court may award an amount sufficient to reimburse the persons aggrieved under subdivision (a) bringing the action for the reasonable expenses incurred by such persons, including attorneys' fees, in connection with the action or proceeding.

(c) A record filed unsigned pursuant to this section is effective without being signed.

(d) Any person, other than a general partner, delivering a record to the Secretary of State for filing, shall state the statutory authority for such action after the signature on the appropriate record.

### California Code Comment
#### By Phil Jelsma

Source—**RULPA Section 205.**

Source—**Cal. Corp. Code § 15625.**

## SECTION 15902.06. DELIVERY TO AND FILING OF RECORDS BY SECRETARY OF STATE; EFFECTIVE TIME AND DATE.

(a) A record authorized or required to be delivered to the Secretary of State for filing under this chapter must be completed on a form prescribed by and in a medium permitted by the Secretary of State, and be delivered to the Secretary of State. Unless the Secretary of State determines that a record does not comply with the filing requirements of this chapter, and if all requisite fees have been paid, the Secretary of State shall file the record.

(b) Except as otherwise provided in Sections 15901.16, 15902.01 and 15902.07, a record delivered to the Secretary of State for filing under this chapter may specify an effective time and delayed effective date. Except as otherwise provided in this chapter, a record filed by the Secretary of State is effective:

(1) if the record does not specify a delayed effective date, on the date the record is filed as evidenced by the Secretary of State's endorsement of the date on the record;

(2) if the record specifies a delayed effective date on the earlier of:

(A) the specified date; or

(B) the 90th day after the record is filed.

(c) In case a delayed effective date is specified, the record may be prevented from becoming effective by a certificate stating that by appropriate action it has been revoked and is null and void, executed in the same manner as the original record and delivered to the Secretary of State for filing before the specified effective date. In the case of certificate of merger, a certificate revoking the earlier filing need only be executed on behalf of one of the constituent parties to the merger. If no such revocation certificate is filed, the record becomes effective on the date specified.

(d) If the Secretary of State determines that a record delivered to the Secretary of State for filing does not conform to the law and returns it to the person delivering it, the record may be resubmitted accompanied by a written opinion of the member of the State Bar of California delivering the record or representing the person delivering it, to the effect that the specific provisions of the record objected to by the Secretary of State do conform to law and stating the points and authorities upon which the opinion is based. The Secretary of State shall rely, with respect to any disputed point of law, other than the application of Sections 15901.08, 15901.09, 15909.02 and 15909.05, upon that written opinion in determining whether the record conforms to law. When filed by the Secretary of State upon resubmission, such record is effective retroactively as of the date that the original record was delivered to the Secretary of State for filing.

## Uniform Limited Partnership Act Comment

**Source**—ULLCA Section 206.

In order for a record prepared by a private person to become part of the public record under this chapter, (i) someone must put a properly prepared version of the record into the possession of the public official specified in the chapter as the appropriate filing officer, and (ii) that filing officer must determine that the record complies with the filing requirements of this chapter and then officially make the record part of the public record. This chapter refers to the first step as delivery to the Secretary of State for filing and refers to the second step as filing. Thus, under this chapter "filing" is an official act.

**Subsection (a)**—The caption need only indicate the title of the record; e.g., Certificate of Limited Partnership, Certificate of Amendment for Limited Partnership.

Filing officers typically note on a filed record the fact, date and time of filing. The copies provided by the filing officer under this subdivision should contain that notation.

This chapter does not provide a remedy if the filing officer wrongfully fails or refuses to file a record.

**Subsection (c)**—This subdivision allows most records to have a delayed effective date, up to 90 days after the date the record is filed by the filing officer. A record specifying a longer delay will not be rejected. Instead, under paragraph (c)(2) and (3), the delayed effective date is adjusted by operation of law to the "90th day after the record is filed." The chapter does not require the filing officer to notify anyone of the adjustment.

## SECTION 15902.07. CORRECTING FILED RECORD.

(a) A limited partnership or foreign limited partnership may deliver to and on a form prescribed by the Secretary of State for filing a certificate of correction to correct a record previously delivered by the limited partnership or foreign limited partnership to the Secretary of State and filed by the Secretary of State, if at the time of filing the record contained false or erroneous information or was defectively signed.

(b) A certificate of correction may not state a delayed effective date and must:

(1) describe the record to be corrected, including its filing date and file number;

(2) specify the incorrect information and the reason it is incorrect or the manner in which the signing was defective; and

(3) correct the incorrect information or defective signature.

(c) When filed by the Secretary of State, a certificate of correction is effective retroactively as of the effective date of the record the certificate corrects, but the certificate is effective when filed:

(1) for the purposes of subdivisions (c) and (d) of Section 15901.03; and

(2) as to persons relying on the uncorrected record and adversely affected by the correction.

### Uniform Limited Partnership Act Comment

**Source**—ULLCA Section 207.

A certificate of correction is appropriate only to correct inaccuracies that existed or signatures that were defective "at the time of filing." A certificate of correction may not be used to correct a record that was accurate when filed but has become inaccurate due to subsequent events.

**Subsection (c)** -Generally, a certificate of correction "relates back." However, there is no retroactive effect: (1) for the purposes of constructive notice under Section 15901.03(c) and (d); and (2) against persons who have relied on the uncorrected record and would be adversely affected if the correction related back.

## SECTION 15902.08. LIABILITY FOR FALSE INFORMATION IN FILED RECORD.

(a) If a record delivered to the Secretary of State for filing under this chapter and filed by the Secretary of State contains false information, a person that suffers loss by reliance on the information may recover damages for the loss from:

(1) a person that signed the record, or caused another to sign it on the person's behalf, and knew the information to be false at the time the record was signed; and

(2) a general partner that has notice that the information was false when the record was filed or has become false because of changed circumstances, if the general partner has notice for a reasonably sufficient time before the information is relied upon to enable the general partner to effect an amendment under Section 15902.02, file a petition pursuant to Section 15902.05, or deliver to the Secretary of State for filing a certificate of correction pursuant to Section 15902.07.

(b) Signing a record authorized or required to be filed under this chapter constitutes an affirmation under the penalties of perjury that the facts stated in the record are true.

### Uniform Limited Partnership Act Comment

This section pertains to both limited partnerships and foreign limited partnerships.

LLLP status is irrelevant to this section. The LLLP shield protects only to the extent that (i) the obligation involved is an obligation of the foreign limited partnership, and (ii) a partner is claimed to be liable for that obligation by reason of being a partner. This section does not address the obligations of a foreign limited partnership and instead imposes direct liability on signers and general partners.

**Subsection (a)**—This subdivision's liability rules apply only to records (i) created by private persons ("delivered to the Secretary of State for filing"), (ii) which actually become part of the public record ("filed by the Secretary of State"). This subdivision does not preempt other law, which might provide remedies for misleading information contained, for example, in a record that is delivered to the filing officer for filing but withdrawn before the filing officer takes the official action of filing the record.

Records filed under this chapter are signed subject to the penalties for perjury. See subdivision (b). This subdivision therefore does not require a party who relies on a record to demonstrate that the reliance was reasonable. Contrast Section 15902.01(d)(2), which provides that, if the partnership agreement is inconsistent with the public record, the public record prevails in favor of a person that is neither a partner nor a transferee and that reasonably relied on the record.

## SECTION 15902.09. REVIVAL OF LIMITED PARTNERSHIP.

(a) A domestic limited partnership whose certificate of limited partnership has been canceled pursuant to Section 15902.03 may be revived by filing with, and on a form prescribed by, the Secretary of State, a certificate of revival. The certificate of revival shall be accompanied by written confirmation by the Franchise Tax Board that all of the following have been paid to the Franchise Tax Board:

(1) The annual tax due under Section 17935 of the Revenue and Taxation Code;

(2) All penalties and interest thereof for each year for which the domestic limited partnership failed to pay such annual tax, including each year between the cancellation of its certificate of limited partnership and its revival.

(b) The certificate of revival shall set forth all of the following:

(1) The name of the limited partnership at the time its certificate of limited partnership was cancelled, and if the name is not available at the time of revival, the name under which the limited partnership is to be revived.

(2) The date of filing of the original certificate of limited partnership.

(3) The address of the limited partnership's designated office.

(4) The name and address of the initial agent for service of process in accordance with paragraph (1) of subdivision (a) of Section 15901.16.

(5) A statement that the certificate of revival is filed by one or more general partners of the limited partnership authorized to execute and file the certificate of revival to revive the limited partnership.

(6) The Secretary of State's file number for the original limited partnership.

(7) The name and address of each general partner.

(8) Any other matters the general partner or partners executing the certificate of revival determine to include therein.

(c) The certificate of revival should be deemed to be an amendment to the certificate of limited partnership, and the limited partnership shall not be required to take any further action to amend its certificate of limited partnership pursuant to Section 15902.02 with respect to the matter set forth in the certificate of revival.

(d) Upon the filing of the certificate of revival, the limited partnership shall be revived with the same force and effect as if the certificate of limited partnership had not been canceled pursuant to Section 15902.03. The revival shall validate all contracts, acts, matters, and things made, done, and performed by the limited partnership, its partners, employees, and agents following the time its certificate of limited partnership was canceled pursuant to Section 15902.03 with the same force and effect and all intents and purposes as if the certificate of limited partnership had remained in full force and effect. This provision shall apply provided that third parties are relying on the acts of the partnership, its partners, employees, and agents. All real and personal property, and all rights and interests, that belong to a limited partnership at the time its certificate of limited partnership was cancelled pursuant to Section 15902.03 or that were acquired by the limited partnership following the cancellation of the certificate of limited partnership, that were not disposed of prior to the time of its revival, shall be vested in the limited partnership after its revival as fully as if they were held by the limited partnership at, and during the time after, as the case may be, the time the certificate of limited partnership was cancelled. After its revival, the limited partnership and its partners shall have all of the same liability for contracts, acts, matters, and things made, done, or performed in the limited partnership's name and on behalf of its partners, employees, and agents, as the limited partnership and its partners would have had if the limited partnership's certificate of limited partnership had at all times remained in full force and effect.

## California Code Comment
### By Phil Jelsma

**Source:** This section is new and permits the limited partnership to revive if the certificate of limited partnership has been cancelled for whatever reason. Revival reinstates any contract or rights from the date of cancellation to the date of revival.

## Article 3.
## LIMITED PARTNERS

**SECTION 15903.01. BECOMING LIMITED PARTNER.** A person becomes a limited partner:

(a) as provided in the partnership agreement;

(b) as the result of a conversion or merger under Article 11 (commencing with Section 15911.01); or

(c) with the consent of all the partners.

### Uniform Limited Partnership Act Comment

**Source**—RULPA Section 301.

Although Section 15908.01(c) contemplates the admission of a limited partner to avoid dissolution, that provision does not itself authorize the admission. Instead, this section controls. Contrast Section 15908.01(c)(2)(B), which itself authorizes the admission of a general partner in order to avoid dissolution.

**SECTION 15903.02. NO RIGHT OR POWER AS LIMITED PARTNER TO BIND LIMITED PARTNERSHIP.** A limited partner does not have the right or the power as a limited partner to act for or bind the limited partnership.

### Uniform Limited Partnership Act Comment

In this respect a limited partner is analogous to a shareholder in a corporation; status as owner provides neither the right to manage nor a reasonable appearance of that right.

The phrase "as a limited partner" is intended to recognize that: (i) this section does not disable a general partner that also owns a limited partner interest, (ii) the partnership agreement may as a matter of contract allocate managerial rights to one or more limited partners; and (iii) a separate agreement can empower and entitle a person that is a limited partner to act for the limited partnership in another capacity; e.g., as an agent. See Comment to Section 15903.05

The fact that a limited partner qua limited partner has no power to bind the limited partnership means that, subject to Section 15901.13 (Dual Capacity), information possessed by a limited partner is not attributed to the limited partnership. See Section 15901.03(h).

This chapter specifies various circumstances in which limited partners have consent rights, including:

- admission of a limited partner, Section 15903.01(c)

- admission of a general partner, Section 15904.01(d)

- amendment of the partnership agreement, Section 15904.06(b)(1)

- the decision to amend the certificate of limited partnership so as to obtain or relinquish LLLP status, Section 15904.06(b)(2)

- the disposition of all or substantially all of the limited partnership's property, outside the ordinary course, Section 15904.06(b)(3)

- the compromise of a partner's obligation to make a contribution or return an improper distribution, Section 15905.02(c)

- expulsion of a limited partner by consent of the other partners, Section 15906.01(b)(4)

- expulsion of a general partner by consent of the other partners, Section 15906.03(d)

- redemption of a transferable interest subject to charging order, using limited partnership property, Section 15907.03(c)(3)

- causing dissolution by consent, Section 15908.01(b)

- causing dissolution by consent following the dissociation of a general partner, when at least one general partner remains, Section 15908.01(c)(2)(A)

- avoiding dissolution and appointing a successor general partner, following the dissociation of the sole general partner, Section 15908.01(c)(2)(B)

- appointing a person to wind up the limited partnership when there is no general partner, Section 15908.03(c)

- approving, amending or abandoning a plan of conversion, Section 15911.03

- approving, amending or abandoning a plan of merger, Section 15911.12.

## SECTION 15903.03. NO LIABILITY AS LIMITED PARTNER FOR LIMITED PARTNERSHIP OBLIGATIONS.

(a) A limited partner is not liable for any obligation of a limited partnership unless named as a general partner in the certificate or, in addition to exercising the rights and powers of a limited partner, the limited partner participates in the control of the business. If a limited partner participates in the control of the business without being named as a general partner, that partner may be held liable as a general partner only to persons who transact business with the limited partnership with actual knowledge of that partner's participation in control and with a reasonable belief, based upon the limited partner's conduct, that the partner is a general partner at the time of the transaction. Nothing in this chapter shall be construed to affect the liability of a limited partner to third parties for the limited partner's participation in tortious conduct.

(b) A limited partner does not participate in the control of the business within the meaning of subdivision (a) solely by doing, attempting to do, or having the right or power to do, one or more of the following:

(1) Being any of the following:

(A) An independent contractor for. an agent or employee of, or transacting business with, the limited partnership or a general partner of the limited partnership.

(B) An officer, director, or shareholder of a corporate general partner of the limited partnership.

(C) A member, manager, or officer of a limited liability company that is a general partner of the limited partnership.

(D) A limited partner of a partnership that is a general partner of the limited partnership.

(E) A trustee, administrator, executor, custodian, or other fiduciary or beneficiary of an estate or trust that is a general partner.

(F) A trustee, officer, advisor, shareholder, or beneficiary of a business trust that is a general partner.

(2) Consulting with and advising a general partner with respect to the business of the limited partnership.

(3) Acting as surety for the limited partnership or for a general partner, guaranteeing one or more specific debts of the limited partnership, providing collateral for the limited partnership or general partner, borrowing money from the limited partnership or a general partner, or lending money to the limited partnership or a general partner.

(4) Approving or disapproving an amendment to the partnership agreement.

(5) Voting on, proposing, or calling a meeting of the partners.

(6) Winding up the partnership pursuant to Section 15908.03.

(7) Executing and filing a certificate pursuant to Section 15902.05, a certificate of withdrawal pursuant to paragraph (12) of subdivision (a) of Section 15902.04 or a certificate of cancellation of certificate of limited partnership pursuant to paragraph (7) of subdivision (a) of Section 15902.04.

(8) Serving on an audit committee or committee performing the functions of an audit committee.

(9) Serving on a committee of the limited partnership or the limited partners for the purpose of approving actions of the general partner.

(10) Calling, requesting, attending, or participating at any meeting of the partners or the limited partners.

(11) Taking any action required or permitted by law to bring, pursue, settle, or terminate a derivative action on behalf of the limited partnership.

(12) Serving on the board of directors or a committee of, consulting with or advising, being or acting as an officer, director, stockholder, partner, member, manager, agent, or employee of, or being or acting as a fiduciary for, any person in which the limited partnership has an interest.

(13) Exercising any right or power permitted to limited partners under this chapter and not specifically enumerated in this subdivision.

(c) The enumeration in subdivision (b) does not mean that any other conduct or the possession or exercise of any other power by a limited partner constitutes participation by the limited partner in the control of the business of the limited partnership.

## Uniform Limited Partnership Act Comment

This section in the Uniform Act provides a full, status-based liability shield for each limited partner, "even if the limited partner participates in the management and control of the limited partnership." The Uniform Act thus eliminates the so-called "control rule" with respect to personal liability for entity obligations and brings limited partners into parity with LLC members, LLP partners and corporate shareholders.

The "control rule" first appeared in an uniform act in 1916, although the concept is much older. Section 7 of the original Uniform Limited Partnership Act provided that "A limited partner shall not become liable as a general partner [*i.e.*, for the obligations of the limited partnership] unless . . . he takes part in the control of the business." The 1976 Uniform Act (ULPA - 1976) "carrie[d] over the basic test from former Section 7," but recognized "the difficulty of determining when the 'control' line has been overstepped." Comment to ULPA-1976, Section 303. Accordingly, ULPA-1976 tried to buttress the limited partner's shield by (i) providing a safe harbor for a lengthy list of activities deemed not to constitute participating in control, ULPA-1976, Section 15903.03(w), and (ii) limiting a limited partner's "control rule" liability "only to persons who transact business with the limited partnership with actual knowledge of [the limited partner's] participation in control." ULPA-1976, Section 303(a). However, these protections were complicated by a countervailing rule which made a limited partner generally liable for the limited partnership's obligations "if the limited partner's participation in the control of the business is . . . substantially the same as the exercise of the powers of a general partner." ULPA-1976, Section 303(a).

The 1985 amendments to ULPA-1976 (*i.e.*, RULPA) further buttressed the limited partner's shield, removing the "substantially the same" rule, expanding the list of safe harbor activities and limiting "control rule" liability "only to persons who transact business with the limited partnership reasonably believing, based upon the limited partner's conduct, that the limited partner is a general partner."

## California Code Comment
### By Phil Jelsma

In a world with LLPs, LLCs and, most importantly, LLLPs, the control rule has become an anachronism. Nevertheless the Senate Judiciary Committee was unwilling to eliminate the control rule and maintained the prior "control rule" liability "only to persons who transact business with the limited partnership reasonably believing, based upon the limited partner's conduct, that the limited partner is a general partner."

## SECTION 15903.04. RIGHT OF LIMITED PARTNER AND FORMER LIMITED PARTNER TO INFORMATION.

(a) On 10 days' demand, made in a record received by the limited partnership, a limited partner may inspect and copy any information required to be maintained pursuant to Section 15901.11 during regular business hours in the limited partnership's designated office. The limited partner need not have any particular purpose for seeking the information.

(b) Subject to subdivision (g), during regular business hours and at a reasonable location specified by the limited partnership, a limited partner may obtain from the limited partnership, which may be transmitted via electronic transmission, and inspect and copy true and full information regarding the state of the activities and financial condition of the limited partnership and other information regarding the activities of the limited partnership as is just and reasonable if:

(1) the limited partner seeks the information for a purpose reasonably related to the partner's interest as a limited partner;

(2) the limited partner makes a demand in a record received by the limited partnership, describing with reasonable particularity the information sought and the purpose for seeking the information; and

(3) the information sought is directly connected to the limited partner's purpose.

(c) Within 10 days after receiving a demand pursuant to subdivision (b), the limited partnership in a record shall inform the limited partner that made the demand:

(1) what information the limited partnership will provide in response to the demand;

(2) when and where the limited partnership will provide the information; and

(3) if the limited partnership declines to provide any demanded information, the limited partnership's reasons for declining.

(d) Subject to subdivision (f), a person dissociated as a limited partner may inspect and copy required information during regular business hours in the limited partnership's designated office if:

(1) the information pertains to the period during which the person was a limited partner;

(2) the person seeks the information in good faith; and

(3) the person meets the requirements of subdivision (b).

(e) The limited partnership shall respond to a demand made pursuant to subdivision (d) in the same manner as provided in subdivision (c).

(f) If a limited partner dies, Section 15907.04 applies.

(g) The limited partnership shall have the right to keep confidential from limited partners for such period of time as the limited partnership deems reasonable, any information which the limited partnership reasonably believes to be in the nature of trade secrets or other information the disclosure of which the limited partnership in good faith believes is not in the best interest of the limited partnership or could damage the limited partnership or its business or which the limited partnership is required by law or by agreement with a third party to keep confidential.

(h) The limited partnership may impose reasonable restrictions on the use of information obtained under this section. In a dispute concerning the reasonableness of a restriction under this subdivision, the limited partnership has the burden of proving reasonableness.

(i) A limited partnership may charge a person that makes a demand under this section reasonable costs of copying, limited to the costs of labor and material.

(j) Whenever this chapter or a partnership agreement provides for a limited partner to give or withhold consent to a matter, before the consent is given or withheld, the limited partnership shall, without demand, provide the limited partner with all information material to the limited partner's decision that the limited partnership knows.

(k) A limited partner or person dissociated as a limited partner may exercise the rights under this section through an attorney or other agent. Any restriction imposed under subdivision (g), subdivision (h) or by the partnership agreement applies both to the attorney or other agent and to the limited partner or person dissociated as a limited partner.

(l) The rights stated in this section do not extend to a person as transferee, but may be exercised by the legal representative of an individual under legal disability who is a limited partner or person dissociated as a limited partner.

## Uniform Limited Partnership Act Comment

This section balances two countervailing concerns relating to information: the need of limited partners and former limited partners for access versus the limited partnership's need to protect confidential business data and other intellectual property. The balance must be understood in the context of fiduciary duties. The general partners are obliged through their duties of care and loyalty to protect information whose confidentiality is important to the limited partnership or otherwise inappropriate for dissemination. See Section 15904.08 (general standards of general partner conduct). A limited partner, in contrast, "does not have any fiduciary duty to the limited partnership or to any other partner solely by reason of being a limited partner." Section 15903.05(a). (Both general partners and limited partners are subject to a duty of good faith and fair dealing. Section 15903.05(b) and 15904.08(d).)

Like predecessor law, this chapter divides limited partner access rights into two categories—required information and other information. However, this chapter builds on predecessor law by:

- expanding slightly the category of required information and stating explicitly that a limited partner may have access to that information without having to show cause

- specifying a procedure for limited partners to follow when demanding access to other information

- specifying how a limited partnership must respond to such a demand and setting a time limit for the response

- retaining predecessor law's "just and reasonable" standard for determining a limited partner's right to other information, while recognizing that, to be "just and reasonable," a limited partner's demand for other information must meet at minimum standards of relatedness and particularity

- expressly requiring the limited partnership to volunteer known, material information when seeking or obtaining consent from limited partners

- codifying (while limiting) the power of the partnership agreement to vary limited partner access rights

- permitting the limited partnership to establish other reasonable limits on access

- providing access rights for former limited partners.

The access rights stated in this section are personal to each limited partner and are enforceable through a direct action under Section 15910.01(a). These access rights are in addition to whatever discovery rights a party has in a civil suit.

**Subsection (a)**—The phrase "required information" is a defined term. See Sections 15901.02(dd) and 15901.11. This subdivision's broad right of access is subject not only to reasonable limitations in the partnership agreement, Section 15901.10(b)(4), but also to the power of the limited partnership to impose reasonable limitations on use. Unless the partnership agreement provides otherwise, it will be the general partner or partners that have the authority to use that power. See Section 15904.06(a).

**Subsection (b)**—The language describing the information to be provided comes essentially verbatim from RULPA Section 305(a)(2)(i) and (iii). The procedural requirements derive from RMBCA Section 16.02(c). This subdivision does not impose a requirement of good faith, because Section 15903.05(b) contains a generally applicable obligation of good faith and fair dealing for limited partners.

**Subsection (d)**—The notion that former owners should have information rights comes from RUPA Section 403(b) and ULLCA Section 408(a). The access is limited to the required information and is subject to certain conditions.

Example: A person dissociated as a limited partner seeks data which the limited partnership has compiled, which relates to the period when the person was a limited partner, but which is beyond the scope of the information required by Section 15901.11. No matter how reasonable the person's purpose and how well drafted the person's demand, the limited partnership is not obliged to provide the data.

Example: A person dissociated as a limited partner seeks access to required information pertaining to the period during which the person was a limited partner. The person makes a bald demand, merely stating a desire to review the required information at the limited partnership's designated office. In particular, the demand does not describe "with reasonable particularity the information sought and the purpose for seeking the information." See subdivision (b)(2). The limited partnership is not obliged to allow access. The person must first comply with subdivision (d), which incorporates by reference the requirements of subdivision (b).

**Subsection (f)** and Section 15907.04 provide greater access rights for the estate of a deceased limited partner.

**Subsection (d)(2)**—A duty of good faith is needed here, because a person claiming access under this subdivision is no longer a limited partner and is no longer subject to Section 15903.05(b). See Section 15906.02(a)(2) (dissociation as a limited partner terminates duty of good faith as to subsequent events).

Subsection (g)—The limited partnership may keep trade secrets confidential from its limited partners.

**Subsection (h)**—This subdivision permits the limited partnership—as distinguished from the partnership agreement—to impose use limitations. Contrast Section 15901.10(b)(4). Under Section 15904.06(a), it will be the general partner or partners that decide whether the limited partnership will impose use restrictions.

The limited partnership bears the burden of proving the reasonableness of any restriction imposed under this subdivision. In determining whether a restriction is reasonable, a court might consider: (i) the danger or other problem the restriction seeks to avoid; (ii) the purpose for which the information is sought; and (iii) whether, in light of both the problem and the purpose, the restriction is reasonably tailored. Restricting use of the names and addresses of limited partners is not per se unreasonable.

The following table compares the limitations available through the partnership agreement with those available under this subdivision.

| | **Partnership Agreement** | **Section 15903.04(g)** |
|---|---|---|
| How restrictions adopted | By the consent of partners when they adopt or amend the partnership agreement, unless the partnership agreement provides another method of amendment | By the general partners, acting under Section 15904.06(a) |
| What restrictions may be imposed | "Reasonable restrictions on the availability and use of information obtained," Section 15901.10(b)(4) | "Reasonable restrictions on the use of information obtained" |
| Burden of proof | The person challenging the restriction must prove that the restriction will "unreasonably restrict the right of information," Section 15901.10(b)(4) | "The limited partnership has the burden of proving reasonableness" |

**Subsection (h)**—Source: RUPA Section 403(b) and ULLCA Section 408(a).

**Subsection (i)**—Source: **ULLCA Section 408(b).**

The duty stated in this subdivision is at the core of the duties owed the limited partners by a limited partnership and its general partners. This subdivision imposes an affirmative duty to volunteer information, but that obligation is limited to information which is both material and known by the limited partnership. The duty applies to known, material information, even if the limited partnership does not know that the information is material.

A limited partnership will "know" what its general partners know. Section 15901.03(h). A limited partnership may also know information known by the "individual conducting the transaction for the [limited partnership]." Section 15901.03(g).

A limited partner's right to information under this subdivision is enforceable through the full panoply of "legal or equitable relief" provided by Section 15910.01(a), including in appropriate circumstances the withdrawal or invalidation of improperly obtained consent and the invalidation or recession of action taken pursuant to that consent.

**Subsection (k)**—Section 15903.04 provides no information rights to a transferee as transferee. Transferee status brings only the very limited information rights stated in Section 15907.02(c).

It is nonetheless possible for a person that happens to be a transferee to have rights under this section. For example, under Section 15906.02(a)(3) a person dissociated as a limited partner becomes a "mere transferee" of its own transferable interest. While that status provides the person no rights under this section, the status of person dissociated as a limited partner triggers rights under subdivision (d).

## SECTION 15903.05. LIMITED DUTIES OF LIMITED PART-NERS.

(a) A limited partner does not have any fiduciary duty to the limited partnership or to any other partner solely by reason of being a limited partner.

(b) A limited partner shall discharge the duties to the partnership and the other partners under this chapter or under the partnership agreement and exercise any rights consistently with the obligation of good faith and fair dealing.

(c) A limited partner does not violate a duty or obligation under this chapter or under the partnership agreement merely because the limited partner's conduct furthers the limited partner's own interest.

### Uniform Limited Partnership Act Comment

**Subsection (a)**—Fiduciary duty typically attaches to a person whose status or role creates significant power for that person over the interests of another person. Under this chapter, limited partners have very limited power of any sort in the regular activities of the limited partnership and no power whatsoever justifying the imposition of fiduciary duties either to the limited partnership or fellow partners. It is possible for a partnership agreement to allocate significant managerial authority and power to a limited partner, but in that case the power exists not as a matter of status or role but rather as a matter of contract. The proper limit on such contract-based power is the obligation of good faith and fair dealing, not fiduciary duty, unless the partnership agreement itself expressly imposes a fiduciary duty or creates a role for a limited partner which, as a matter of other law, gives rise to a fiduciary duty. For example, if the partnership agreement makes a limited partner an agent for the limited partnership as to particular matters, the law of agency will impose fiduciary duties on the limited partner with respect to the limited partner's role as agent.

**Subsection (b)**—Source: RUPA Section 404(d). The same language appears in Section 15904.08(d), pertaining to general partners.

The obligation of good faith and fair dealing is not a fiduciary duty, does not command altruism or self-abnegation, and does not prevent a partner from acting in the partner's own self-interest. Courts should not use the obligation to change ex post facto the parties' or this chapter's allocation of risk and power. To the contrary, in light of the nature of a limited partnership, the obligation should be used only to protect agreed-upon arrangements from conduct that is manifestly beyond what a reasonable person could have contemplated when the arrangements were made.

The partnership agreement or this chapter may grant discretion to a partner, and that partner may properly exercise that discretion even though another partner suffers as a consequence. Conduct does not violate the obligation of good faith and fair dealing merely because that conduct substantially prejudices a party. Indeed, parties allocate risk precisely because prejudice may occur. The exercise of discretion constitutes a breach of the obligation of good faith and fair dealing only when the party claiming breach shows that the conduct has no honestly-held purpose that legitimately comports with the parties' agreed-upon arrangements. Once such a purpose appears, courts should not second guess a party's choice of method in serving that purpose, unless the party invoking the obligation of good faith and fair dealing shows that the choice of method itself lacks any honestly-held purpose that legitimately comports with the parties' agreed-upon arrangements.

In sum, the purpose of the obligation of good faith and fair dealing is to protect the arrangement the partners have chosen for themselves, not to restructure that arrangement under the guise of safeguarding it.

## SECTION 15903.06. PERSON ERRONEOUSLY BELIEVING SELF TO BE LIMITED PARTNER.

(a) Except as otherwise provided in subdivision (b), a person that makes an investment in a business enterprise and erroneously but in good faith believes that the person has become a limited partner in the enterprise is not liable for the enterprise's obligations by reason of making the investment, receiving distributions from the enterprise, or exercising any rights of or appropriate to a limited partner, if, on ascertaining the mistake, the person:

(1) causes an appropriate certificate of limited partnership, amendment, or certificate of correction to be signed and delivered to the Secretary of State for filing; or

(2) withdraws from future participation as an owner in the enterprise by signing and delivering to and on a form prescribed by the Secretary of State for filing a certificate of withdrawal under this section.

(b) A person that makes an investment described in subdivision (a) is liable to the same extent as a general partner to any third party that enters into a transaction with the enterprise, believing in good faith that the person is a general partner, before the Secretary of State files a certificate of withdrawal, certificate of limited partnership, amendment, or certificate of correction to show that the person is not a general partner.

(c) If a person makes a diligent effort in good faith to comply with paragraph (1) of subdivision (a) and is unable to cause the appropriate certificate of limited partnership, amendment, or certificate of correction to be signed and delivered to the Secretary of State for filing, the person has the right to withdraw from the enterprise pursuant to paragraph (2) of subdivision (a) even if the withdrawal would otherwise breach an agreement with others that are or have agreed to become co-owners of the enterprise.

### Uniform Limited Partnership Act Comment

Source—RULPA Section 304, substantially redrafted for reasons of style.

## SECTION 15903.07. CLASSES; TERMS OF AGREEMENT; RIGHT TO VOTE.

(a) The partnership agreement may provide for the creation of classes of limited partners. The partnership agreement shall define the rights, powers, and duties of those classes, including rights, powers, and duties senior to other classes of limited partners.

(b) The partnership agreement may provide to all or certain specified classes of limited partners the right to vote separately or with all or any class or the general partners on any matter.

### California Code Comment
#### By Phil Jelsma

Source—California Corporations Code § 15631.5.

## ARTICLE 4.
## GENERAL PARTNERS

## SECTION 15904.01. BECOMING GENERAL PARTNER.

A person becomes a general partner:

(a) as provided in the partnership agreement:

(b) under paragraph (2) of subdivision (c) of Section 15908.01 following the dissociation of a limited partnership's last general partner;

(c) as the result of a conversion or merger under Article 11 (commencing with Section 15911.01); or

(d) with the consent of all the partners.

## Uniform Limited Partnership Act Comment

This section does not make a person's status as a general partner dependent on the person being so designated in the certificate of limited partnership. If a person does become a general partner under this section without being so designated:

- the limited partnership is obligated to promptly and appropriately amend the certificate of limited partnership, Section 15902.02(b)(1);

- each general partner that knows of the anomaly is personally obligated to cause the certificate to be promptly and appropriately amended, Section 15902.02(c)(1), and is subject to liability for failing to do so, Section 15902.08(a)(2);

- the "non-designated" general partner has:

  - all the rights and duties of a general partner to the limited partnership and the other partners, and

  - the powers of a general partner to bind the limited partnership under Sections 15904.02 and 15904.03, but

  - no power to sign records which are to be filed on behalf of the limited partnership under this chapter.

Example: By consent of the partners of XYZ limited partnership, G is admitted as a general partner. However, XYZ's certificate of limited partnership is not amended accordingly. Later, G—acting without actual authority—purports to bind XYZ to a transaction with Third Party. Third Party does not review the filed certificate of limited partnership before entering into the transaction. XYZ might be bound under Section 15904.02.

**Section 15904.02** attributes to a limited partnership "[a]n act of a general partner for apparently carrying on in the ordinary course the limited partnership's activities or activities of the kind carried on by the limited partnership." The limited partnership's liability under Section 15904.02 does not depend on the "act of a general partner" being the act of a general partner designated in the certificate of limited partnership. Moreover, the notice provided by Section 15901.03(c) does not undercut G's appearance of authority. Section 15904.02 refers only to notice under Section 15901.03(d) and, in any event, according to the second sentence of Section 15901.03(c), the fact that a person is not listed as in the certificate as a general partner is not notice that the person is not a general partner. See Comment to Section 15901.03(c).

Example: Same facts, except that Third Party does review the certificate of limited partnership before entering into the transaction. The result might still be the same.

The omission of a person's name from the certificate's list of general partners is not notice that the person is not a general partner. Therefore, Third Party's review of the certificate does not mean that Third Party knew, had received a notification or had notice that G lacked authority. At most, XYZ could argue that, because Third Party knew that G was not listed in the certificate, a transaction entered into by G could not appear to Third Party to be for apparently carrying on the limited partnership's activities in the ordinary course.

There is no requirement that a general partner have an interest in partnership capital, profits, losses or distributions. This is consistent with existing laws where interests in profits, losses and distributions are based on contributions. If the general partner does not make any contributions to the partnership, it would not have any interest in profit, losses and distributions.

## SECTION 15904.02. GENERAL PARTNER AGENT OF LIMITED PARTNERSHIP.

(a) Each general partner is an agent of the limited partnership for the purposes of its activities. An act of a general partner, including the signing of a record in the partnership's name, for apparently carrying on in the ordinary course the limited partnership's activities or activities of the kind carried on by the limited partnership binds the limited partnership, unless the general partner did not have authority to act for the limited partnership in the particular matter and the person with which the general partner was dealing knew, had received a notification, or had notice under subdivision (d) of Section 15901.03 that the general partner lacked authority.

(b) An act of a general partner which is not apparently for carrying on in the ordinary course the limited partnership's activities or activities of the kind carried on by the limited partnership binds the limited partnership only if the act was actually authorized by all the other partners.

### Uniform Limited Partnership Act Comment

**Source**—RUPA Section 301. For the meaning of "authority" in subdivision (a) and "authorized" in subdivision (b), see RUPA Section 301, Comment 3 (stating that "Subsection (2) of RUPA Section 301 makes it clear that the partnership is bound by a partner's actual authority, even if the partner has no apparent authority"; emphasis added).

The fact that a person is not listed in the certificate of limited partnership as a general partner is not notice that the person is not a partner and is not notice that the person lacks authority to act for the limited partnership. See Comment to Section 15901.03(c) and Comment to Section 15904.01.

**Section 15901.03(f)** defines receipt of notification. Section 15901.03(d) lists various public filings, each of which provides notice 90 days after its effective date.

Example: For the past ten years, X has been a general partner of XYZ limited partnership and has regularly conducted the limited partnership's business with Third Party. However, 100 days ago the limited partnership expelled X as a general partner and the next day delivered for filing an amendment to XYZ's certificate of limited partnership which stated that X was no longer a general partner. On that same day, the filing officer filed the amendment.

Today X approaches Third Party, purports still be to a general partner of XYZ and purports to enter into a transaction with Third Party on XYZ's behalf. Third

Party is unaware that X has been expelled and has no reason to doubt that X's bona fides. Nonetheless, XYZ is not liable on the transaction. Under Section 15901.03(d), Third Party has notice that X is dissociated and perforce has notice that X is not a general partner authorized to bind XYZ.

## SECTION 15904.03. LIMITED PARTNERSHIP LIABLE FOR GENERAL PARTNER'S ACTIONABLE CONDUCT.

(a) A limited partnership is liable for loss or injury caused to a person, or for a penalty incurred, as a result of a wrongful act or omission, or other actionable conduct, of a general partner acting in the ordinary course of activities of the limited partnership or with authority of the limited partnership.

(b) If, in the course of the limited partnership's activities or while acting with authority of the limited partnership, a general partner receives or causes the limited partnership to receive money or property of a person not a partner, and the money or property is misapplied by a general partner, the limited partnership is liable for the loss.

### Uniform Limited Partnership Act Comment

**Source**—RUPA Section 305. For the meaning of "authority" in subdivisions (a) and (b), see RUPA Section 305, Comment. The third-to-last paragraph of that Comment states:

The partnership is liable for the actionable conduct or omission of a partner acting in the ordinary course of its business or "with the authority of the partnership." This is intended to include a partner's apparent, as well as actual, authority, thereby bringing within Section 305(a) the situation covered in UPA Section 14(a).

The last paragraph of that Comment states:

Section 305(b) is drawn from UPA Section 14(b), but has been edited to improve clarity. It imposes strict liability on the partnership for the misapplication of money or property received by a partner in the course of the partnership's business or otherwise within the scope of the partner's actual authority.

**Section 15904.03(a)** of this chapter is taken essentially verbatim from RUPA Section 15903.05(a), and Section 15904.03(b) of this chapter is taken essentially verbatim from RUPA Section 15903.05(b).

This section makes the limited partnership vicariously liable for a partner's misconduct. That vicariously liability in no way discharges or diminishes the partner's direct liability for the partner's own misconduct.

A general partner can cause a limited partnership to be liable under this section, even if the general partner is not designated as a general partner in the certificate of limited partnership. See Comment to Section 15904.01.

## SECTION 15904.04. GENERAL PARTNER'S LIABILITY.

(a) Except as otherwise provided in subdivision (b), all general partners are liable jointly and severally for all obligations of the limited partnership unless otherwise agreed by the claimant or provided by law.

(b) A person that becomes a general partner of an existing limited partnership is not personally liable for an obligation of a limited partnership incurred before the person became a general partner.

## Uniform Limited Partnership Act Comment

**Source**—RUPA Section 306.

Following RUPA and the UPA, this chapter leaves to other law the question of when a limited partnership obligation is incurred.

## California Code Comment
### By Phil Jelsma

The Assembly Judiciary Committee elected not to provide that limited liability limited partnerships (LLLPs) could be formed under California law but this chapter does allow foreign limited liability partnerships to register to do business in California as a foreign limited partnership.

## SECTION 15904.05. ACTIONS BY AND AGAINST PARTNERSHIP AND PARTNERS.

(a) To the extent not inconsistent with Section 15904.04, a general partner may be joined in an action against the limited partnership or named in a separate action.

(b) A judgment against a limited partnership is not by itself a judgment against a general partner. A judgment against a limited partnership may not be satisfied from a general partner's assets unless there is also a judgment against the general partner.

(c) A judgment creditor of a general partner may not levy execution against the assets of the general partner to satisfy a judgment based on a claim against the limited partnership, unless the partner is personally liable for the claim under Section 15904.04 and:

(1) a judgment based on the same claim has been obtained against the limited partnership and a writ of execution on the judgment has been returned unsatisfied in whole or in part;

(2) the limited partnership is a debtor in bankruptcy;

(3) the general partner has agreed that the creditor need not exhaust limited partnership assets;

(4) a court grants permission to the judgment creditor to levy execution against the assets of a general partner based on a finding that limited partnership assets subject to execution are clearly insufficient to satisfy the judgment, that exhaustion of limited partnership

assets is excessively burdensome, or that the grant of permission is an appropriate exercise of the court's equitable powers; or

(5) liability is imposed on the general partner by law or contract independent of the existence of the limited partnership.

## Uniform Limited Partnership Act Comment

Source—RUPA **Section 307.**

## SECTION 15904.06. MANAGEMENT RIGHTS OF GENERAL PARTNER.

(a) Each general partner has equal rights in the management and conduct of the limited partnership's activities. Except as expressly provided in this chapter, any matter relating to the activities of the limited partnership may be exclusively decided by the general partner or, if there is more than one general partner, by a majority of the general partners.

(b) The consent of each partner is necessary to:

(1) amend the partnership agreement; and

(2) sell, lease, exchange, or otherwise dispose of all, or substantially all, of the limited partnership's property, with or without the good will, other than in the usual and regular course of the limited partnership's activities.

(c) A limited partnership shall reimburse a general partner for payments made and indemnify a general partner for liabilities incurred by the general partner in the ordinary course of the activities of the partnership or for the preservation of its activities or property.

(d) A limited partnership shall reimburse a general partner for an advance to the limited partnership beyond the amount of capital the general partner agreed to contribute.

(e) A payment or advance made by a general partner which gives rise to an obligation of the limited partnership under subdivision (c) or (d) constitutes a loan to the limited partnership which accrues interest from the date of the payment or advance.

(f) A general partner is not entitled to remuneration for services performed for the partnership.

## Uniform Limited Partnership Act Comment

**Source**—RUPA Section 401 and ULLCA Section 404.

**Subsection (a)**—As explained in the Prefatory Note, this chapter assumes that, more often than not, people utilizing the chapter will want (i) strong centralized management, strongly entrenched, and (ii) passive investors with little control over the entity. Section 15903.02 essentially excludes limited partners from the ordinary management of a limited partnership's activities. This subdivision states affirmatively the general partners' commanding role. Only the partnership agreement and the express provisions of this chapter can limit that role.

The authority granted by this subdivision includes the authority to delegate. Delegation does not relieve the delegating general partner or partners of their duties under Section 15904.08. However, the fact of delegation is a fact relevant to any breach of duty analysis.

Example: A sole general partner personally handles all "important paperwork" for a limited partnership. The general partner neglects to renew the fire insurance coverage on the a building owned by the limited partnership, despite having received and read a warning notice from the insurance company. The building subsequently burns to the ground and is a total loss. The general partner might be liable for breach of the duty of care under Section 15904.08(c) (gross negligence).

Example: A sole general partner delegates responsibility for insurance renewals to the limited partnership's office manager, and that manager neglects to renew the fire insurance coverage on the building. Even assuming that the office manager has been grossly negligent, the general partner is not necessarily liable under Section 15904.08(c). The office manager's gross negligence is not automatically attributed to the general partner. Under Section 15904.08(c), the question is whether the general partner was grossly negligent (or worse) in selecting the general manager, delegating insurance renewal matters to the general manager and supervising the general manager after the delegation.

For the consequences of delegating authority to a person that is a limited partner, see the Comment to Section 15903.05.

The partnership agreement may also provide for delegation and, subject to Section 15901.10(b)(5)—(7), may modify a general partner's Section 15904.08 duties.

**Subsection (b)**—This subdivision limits the managerial rights of the general partners, requiring the consent of each general and limited partner for the specified actions. The subdivision is subject to change by the partnership agreement, except as provided in Section 15901.10(b)(12) (pertaining to consent rights established by Section 15911.10).

**Subsection (c)**—This chapter does not include any parallel provision for limited partners, because they are assumed to be passive. To the extent that by contract or other arrangement a limited partner has authority to act on behalf of the limited partnership, agency law principles will create an indemnity obligation. In other situations, principles of restitution might apply.

**Subsection (f)**—Unlike RUPA Section 401(h), this subdivision provides no compensation for winding up efforts. In a limited partnership, winding up is one of the tasks for which the limited partners depend on the general partner. There is no reason for the chapter to single out this particular task as giving rise to compensation.

## SECTION 15904.07. RIGHT OF GENERAL PARTNER AND FORMER GENERAL PARTNER TO INFORMATION.

(a) A general partner, without having any particular purpose for seeking the information, may inspect and copy during regular business hours:

(1) in the limited partnership's designated office, required information; and

(2) at a reasonable location specified by the limited partnership, any other records maintained by the limited partnership regarding the limited partnership's activities and financial condition.

(b) Each general partner and the limited partnership shall furnish to a general partner which may be transmitted via electronic transmission:

(1) without demand, any information concerning the limited partnership's activities and activities reasonably required for the proper exercise of the general partner's rights and duties under the partnership agreement or this chapter; and

(2) on demand, any other information concerning the limited partnership's activities, except to the extent the demand or the information demanded is unreasonable or otherwise improper under the circumstances.

(c) Subject to subdivision (e), on 10 days' demand made in a record received by the limited partnership, a person dissociated as a general partner may have access to the information and records described in subdivision (a) at the location specified in subdivision (a) if:

(1) the information or record pertains to the period during which the person was a general partner;

(2) the person seeks the information or record in good faith; and

(3) the person satisfies the requirements imposed on a limited partner by subdivision (b) of Section 15903.04.

(d) The limited partnership shall respond to a demand made pursuant to subdivision (c) in the same manner as provided in subdivision (c) of Section 15903.04.

(e) If a general partner dies, Section 15907.04 applies.

(f) The limited partnership may impose reasonable restrictions on the use of information under this section. In any dispute concerning the reasonableness of a restriction under this subdivision, the limited partnership has the burden of proving reasonableness.

(g) A limited partnership may charge a person dissociated as a general partner that makes a demand under this section reasonable costs of copying, limited to the costs of labor and material.

(h) A general partner or person dissociated as a general partner may exercise the rights under this section through an attorney or other agent. Any restriction imposed under subdivision (f) or by the partnership agreement applies both to the attorney or other agent and to the general partner or person dissociated as a general partner.

(i) The rights under this section do not extend to a person as transferee, but the rights under subdivision (c) of a person dissociated as a general partner may be exercised by the legal representative of an individual who dissociated as a general partner under paragraph (2) or (3) of subdivision (g) of Section 15906.03.

## Uniform Limited Partnership Act Comment

This section's structure parallels the structure of Section 15903.04 and the Comment to that section may be helpful in understanding this section.

**Subsection (b)**—Source: RUPA Section 403(c).

**Subsection (b)(1)**—If a particular item of material information is apparent in the limited partnership's records, whether a general partner is obliged to disseminate that information to fellow general partners depends on the circumstances.

Example: A limited partnership has two general partners: each of which is regularly engaged in conducting the limited partnership's activities; both of which are aware of and have regular access to all significant limited partnership records; and neither of which has special responsibility for or knowledge about any particular aspect of those activities or the partnership records pertaining to any particular aspect of those activities. Most likely, neither general partner is obliged to draw the other general partner's attention to information apparent in the limited partnership's records.

Example: Although a limited partnership has three general partners, one is the managing partner with day-to-day responsibility for running the limited partnership's activities. The other two meet periodically with the managing general partner, and together with that partner function in a manner analogous to a corporate board of directors. Most likely, the managing general partner has a duty to draw the attention of the other general partners to important information, even if that information would be apparent from a review of the limited partnership's records.

In all events under subdivision (b)(1), the question is whether the disclosure by one general partner is "reasonably required for the proper exercise" of the other general partner's rights and duties.

**Subsection (f)**—This provision is identical to Section 15903.04(g) and the Comment to Section 15903.04(g) is applicable here. Under this chapter, general and limited partners have sharply different roles. A restriction that is reasonable as to a limited partner is not necessarily reasonable as to a general partner.

**Subsection (g)**—No charge is allowed for current general partners, because in almost all cases they would be entitled to reimbursement under Section 15904.06(c). Contrast Section 15903.04(h), which authorizes charges to current limited partners.

**Subsection (i)**—The Comment to Section 15903.04(k) is applicable here.

## SECTION 15904.08. GENERAL STANDARDS OF GENERAL PARTNER'S CONDUCT.

(a) The fiduciary duties that a general partner owes to the limited partnership and the other partners are the duties of loyalty and care under subdivisions (b) and (c).

(b) A general partner's duty of loyalty to the limited partnership and the other partners is limited to the following:

(1) to account to the limited partnership and hold as trustee for it any property, profit, or benefit derived by the general partner in the conduct and winding up of the limited partnership's activities or derived from a use by the general partner of limited partnership property, including the appropriation of a limited partnership opportunity;

(2) to refrain from dealing with the limited partnership in the conduct or winding up of the limited partnership's activities as or on behalf of a party having an interest adverse to the limited partnership; and

(3) to refrain from competing with the limited partnership in the conduct or winding up of the limited partnership's activities.

(c) A general partner's duty of care to the limited partnership and the other partners in the conduct and winding up of the limited partnership's activities is limited to refraining from engaging in grossly negligent or reckless conduct, intentional misconduct, or a knowing violation of law.

(d) A general partner shall discharge the duties to the partnership and the other partners under this chapter or under the partnership agreement and exercise any rights consistently with the obligation of good faith and fair dealing.

(e) A general partner does not violate a duty or obligation under this chapter or under the partnership agreement merely because the general partner's conduct furthers the general partner's own interest.

### Uniform Limited Partnership Act Comment

**Source**—RUPA Section 404

This section does not prevent a general partner from delegating one or more duties, but delegation does not discharge the duty. For further discussion, see the Comment to Section 15904.06.

## SECTION 15904.09. CLASSES OF GENERAL PARTNERS.

(a) A partnership agreement may provide for the creation of classes of general partners. The partnership agreement shall define the rights, powers, and duties of those classes including rights, powers, and duties senior to other classes of general partners.

(b) The partnership agreement may provide to all or certain specified classes of general partners the right to vote separately or with all or any class of the general partners on any matters.

### California Code Comment
*By Phil Jelsma*

Source—California Corporations Code § 15645.

## ARTICLE 5.
## CONTRIBUTIONS AND DISTRIBUTIONS

**SECTION 15905.01. FORM OF CONTRIBUTION.** A contribution of a partner may consist of tangible or intangible property or other benefit to the limited partnership, including money, services performed, promissory notes, other agreements to contribute cash or property, and contracts for services to be performed.

### Uniform Limited Partnership Act Comment

Source—ULLCA Section 401.

**SECTION 15905.02. LIABILITY FOR CONTRIBUTION.**

(a) A partner's obligation to contribute money or other property or other benefit to, or to perform services for, a limited partnership is not excused by the partner's death, disability, or other inability to perform personally.

(b) If a partner does not make a promised nonmonetary contribution, the partner is obligated at the option of the limited partnership to contribute money equal to the value of that portion, as stated in the required information, of the stated contribution which has not been made.

(c) The obligation of a partner to make a contribution or return money or other property paid or distributed in violation of this chapter may be compromised only by consent of all partners. A creditor of a limited partnership which extends credit or otherwise acts in reliance on an obligation described in subdivision (a), without notice of any compromise under this subdivision, may enforce the original obligation.

(d) A partnership agreement may provide that the interest of a partner who fails to make any contribution or other payment that the partner is required to make will be subject to specific remedies for, or specific consequences of, the failure. A provision shall be enforceable in accordance with its terms unless the partner seeking to invalidate the provision establishes that the provision was unreasonable under the circumstances existing at the time the agreement was made. The specific remedies or consequences may include loss of voting, approval, or other rights, loss of the partner's ability to actively participate in the management and operations of the partnership, liquidated damages, or a reduction of the defaulting partner's economic rights. The reduction of the defaulting partner's economic rights may include one or more of the following provisions:

(1) Diluting, reducing or eliminating the defaulting partner's proportionate interest in the partnership.

(2) Subordinating the defaulting partner's interest in the partnership to that of nondefaulting partners.

(3) Permitting a forced sale of the partnership interest.

(4) Permitting the lending or contribution by other partners of the amount necessary to meet the defaulting partner's commitment.

(5) Adjusting the interest rates or other rates of return, preferred, priority, or otherwise, with respect to contributions by or capital accounts of the other partners.

(6) Fixing the value of the defaulting partner's interest in the partnership by appraisal, formula and redemption, or sale of the defaulting partner's interest in the partnership at a percentage of that value.

(7) Nothing in this section shall be construed to affect the rights of third-party creditors of the partnership to seek equitable remedies nor any rights existing under the Uniform Fraudulent Transfer Act (Chapter 1 (commencing with Section 3439)of Title 2 of Part 2 of Division 4 of the Civil Code).

## Uniform Limited Partnership Act Comment

In contrast with predecessor law, RULPA Section 502(a), this chapter does not include a statute of frauds provision covering promised contributions. Section 15901.11(8)(A) does require that the value of a promised contribution be memorialized, but that requirement does not affect enforceability. See Comment to Section 15901.11(8).

**Subsection (a)**—Source: RULPA Section 502(b).

Under common law principles of impracticability, an individual's death or incapacity will sometimes discharge a duty to render performance. Restatement

(Second) of Contracts, Sections 261 and 262. This subdivision overrides those principles.

**Subsection (b)**—RULPA Section 502(b).

This subdivision is a statutory liquidated provision, exercisable at the option of the limited partnership, with the damage amount set according to the value of the promised, non-monetary contribution as stated in the required information.

Example: In order to become a limited partner, a person promises to contribute to the limited partnership various assets which the partnership agreement values at $150,000. In return for the person's promise, and in light of the agreed value, the limited partnership admits the person as a limited partner with a right to receive 25% of the limited partnership's distributions.

The promised assets are subject to a security agreement, but the limited partner promises to contribute them "free and clear." Before the limited partner can contribute the assets, the secured party forecloses on the security interest and sells the assets at a public sale for $75,000. Even the $75,000 reflects the actual fair market value of the assets, under this subdivision the limited partnership has a claim against the limited partner for "the value, as stated in the required information, of the stated contribution which has not been made"—*i.e.*, $150,000.

This section applies "at the option of the limited partnership" and does not affect other remedies which the limited partnership may have under other law.

Example: Same facts as the previous example, except that the public sale brings $225,000. The limited partnership is not obliged to invoke this subdivision and may instead sue for breach of the promise to make the contribution, asserting the $225,000 figure as evidence of the actual loss suffered as a result of the breach.

**Subsection (c)**—Source: ULLCA Section 402(b); RULPA Section 502(c). The first sentence of this subdivision applies not only to promised contributions but also to improper distributions. See Sections 15905.08 and 15905.09. The second sentence, pertaining to creditor's rights, applies only to promised contributions.

## California Code Comment
### By Phil Jelsma

**Subsection (d)**—Cal. Corp. Code Section 17201(a)(3).

# SECTION 15905.03. SHARING OF DISTRIBUTIONS. A distribution by a limited partnership must be shared among the partners on the basis of the value, as stated in the required records when the limited partnership decides to make the distribution, of the contributions the limited partnership has received from each partner.

## Uniform Limited Partnership Act Comment

In the absence of an agreement as to distributions, the chapter provides that distributions are to be made in accordance with each partner's relative contributions to the partnership no matter the form of the contribution. The Uniform Act made distributions based on the value of contributions, but the Drafting Committee thought that valuation is a difficult, subjective process and it would be preferable for the partners to determine the relative weight of their contributions.

**SECTION 15905.035. ALLOCATION OF PROFITS AND LOSSES.** The profits and losses of a limited partnership shall be allocated among the partners in the manner provided in the partnership agreement. If the partnership agreement does not otherwise provide, profits and losses shall be allocated in the same manner as the partners share distributions.

### California Code Comment
#### By Phil Jelsma

The Uniform Act contains no rules on the allocations of profits and losses, generally deferring to the tax rules of Section 704 of the Internal Revenue Code. The Drafting Committee thought it was preferable to provide a default rule rather than no standard for distribution. Section 15905.035 continues the rule found in Cal Corp Code 15653. Since the general partner may elect to not make a contribution, a general partner may have no interest in profits, losses or distributions under this Section and Section 15905.03.

**SECTION 15905.04. INTERIM DISTRIBUTIONS.** A partner does not have a right to any distribution before the dissolution and winding up of the limited partnership unless the limited partnership decides to make an interim distribution.

### Uniform Limited Partnership Act Comment

Under Section 15904.06(a), the general partner or partners make this decision for the limited partnership.

**SECTION 15905.05. NO DISTRIBUTION ON ACCOUNT OF DISSOCIATION.** A person does not have a right to receive a distribution on account of dissociation.

### Uniform Limited Partnership Act Comment

This section varies substantially from predecessor law. RULPA Sections 603 and 604 permitted a limited partner to withdraw on six months notice and receive the fair value of the limited partnership interest, unless the partnership agreement provided the limited partner with some exit right or stated a definite duration for the limited partnership.

Under this chapter, a partner that dissociates becomes a transferee of its own transferable interest. See Sections 15906.02(a)(3) (person dissociated as a limited partner) and 15906.05(a)(5) (person dissociated as a general partner).

**SECTION 15905.06. DISTRIBUTION IN KIND.** A partner does not have a right to demand or receive any distribution from a limited partnership in any form other than cash. Subject to subdivision (b) of Section 15905.08, a limited partnership may distribute an asset in kind to the extent each partner receives a percentage of the asset equal to the partner's share of distributions.

## Uniform Limited Partnership Act Comment

Source—RULPA Section 605.

**SECTION 15905.07. RIGHT TO DISTRIBUTION.** When a partner or transferee becomes entitled to receive a distribution, the partner or transferee has the status of, and is entitled to all remedies available to, a creditor of the limited partnership with respect to the distribution. However, the limited partnership's obligation to make a distribution is subject to offset for any amount owed to the limited partnership by the partner or dissociated partner on whose account the distribution is made.

## Uniform Limited Partnership Act Comment

Source—RULPA Section 606.

This section's first sentence refers to distributions generally. Contrast Section 15905.08(e), which refers to indebtedness issued as a distribution.

The reference in the second sentence to "dissociated partner" encompasses circumstances in which the partner is gone and the dissociated partner's transferable interest is all that remains.

## SECTION 15905.08. LIMITATIONS ON DISTRIBUTION.

(a) A limited partnership may not make a distribution in violation of the partnership agreement.

(b) A limited partnership may not make a distribution if after the distribution:

(1) the limited partnership would not be able to pay its debts as they become due in the ordinary course of the limited partnership's activities; or

(2) the limited partnership's total assets would be less than the sum of its total liabilities plus the amount that would be needed, if the limited partnership were to be dissolved, wound up, and terminated at the time of the distribution, to satisfy the preferential rights upon dissolution, winding up, and termination of partners whose preferential rights are superior to those of persons receiving the distribution.

(c) A limited partnership may base a determination that a distribution is not prohibited under subdivision (b) on financial statements prepared on the basis of accounting practices and principles that are reasonable in the circumstances or on a fair valuation or other method that is reasonable in the circumstances.

(d) Except as otherwise provided in subdivision (g), the effect of a distribution under subdivision (b) is measured:

(1) in the case of distribution by purchase, redemption, or other acquisition of a transferable interest in the limited partnership, as of the date money or other property is transferred or debt incurred by the limited partnership; and

(2) in all other cases, as of the date:

(A) the distribution is authorized, if the payment occurs within 120 days after that date; or

(B) the payment is made, if payment occurs more than 120 days after the distribution is authorized.

(e) A limited partnership's indebtedness to a partner incurred by reason of a distribution made in accordance with this section is at parity with the limited partnership's indebtedness to its general unsecured creditors.

(f) A limited partnership's indebtedness, including indebtedness issued in connection with or as part of a distribution, is not considered a liability for purposes of subdivision (b) if the terms of the indebtedness provide that payment of principal and interest are made only to the extent that a distribution could then be made to partners under this section.

(g) If indebtedness is issued as a distribution, each payment of principal or interest on the indebtedness is treated as a distribution, the effect of which is measured on the date the payment is made.

## Uniform Limited Partnership Act Comment

**Source**—ULLCA Section 406. See also RMBCA Section 6.40. Reasonable compensation to partners for past or present services or contributions to profit sharing or contributions to retirement plans, pension plans or other benefit programs should not be treated as a distribution for purposes of this Section and Section 15905.09.

**Subsection (c)**—This subdivision appears to impose a standard of ordinary care, in contrast with the general duty of care stated in Section 15904.08(c). For a reconciliation of these two provisions, see Comment to Section 15905.09(a).

## SECTION 15905.09. LIABILITY FOR IMPROPER DISTRIBUTIONS.

(a) A general partner that consents to a distribution made in violation of Section 15905.08 is personally liable to the limited partnership for the amount of the distribution which exceeds the amount that could have been distributed without the violation if it is established that in consenting to the distribution the general partner failed to comply with Section 15905.08.

(b) A partner or transferee that received a distribution knowing that the distribution to that partner or transferee was made in violation of Section 15905.08 is personally liable to the limited partnership but only to the extent that the distribution received by the partner or transferee exceeded the amount that could have been properly paid under Section 15905.08.

(c) A general partner against which an action is commenced under subdivision (a) may:

(1) implead in the action any other person that is liable under subdivision (a) and compel contribution from the person; and

(2) implead in the action any person that received a distribution in violation of subdivision (b) and compel contribution from the person in the amount the person received in violation of subdivision (b).

(d) An action under this section is barred if it is not commenced within four years after the distribution.

## Uniform Limited Partnership Act Comment

**Source**—ULLCA Section 407. See also RMBCA Section 8.33.

In substance and effect this section protects the interests of creditors of the limited partnership. Therefore, according to Section 15901.10(b)(13), the partnership agreement may not change this section in a way that restricts the rights of those creditors. As for a limited partnership's power to compromise a claim under this section, see Section 15905.02(c).

**Subsection (a)**—This subdivision refers both to Section 15905.08, which includes in its subdivision (c) a standard of ordinary care ("reasonable in the circumstances"), and to Section 15904.08, which includes in its subdivision (c) a general duty of care that is limited to "refraining from engaging in grossly negligent or reckless conduct, intentional misconduct, or a knowing violation of law."

A limited partnership's failure to meet the standard of Section 15905.08(c) cannot by itself cause a general partner to be liable under Section 15905.09(a). Both of the following would have to occur before a failure to satisfy Section 15905.08(c) could occasion personal liability for a general partner under Section 15905.09(a):

the limited partnership "bases a determination that a distribution is not prohibited . . . on financial statements prepared on the basis of accounting practices and principles that are [not] reasonable in the circumstances or on a not fair valuation or other method that is [not] reasonable in the circumstances" [Section 15905.08(c)]

AND

the general partner's decision to rely on the improper methodology in consenting to the distribution constitutes "grossly negligent or reckless conduct, intentional misconduct, or a knowing violation of law" [Section 15904.08(c)] or breaches some other duty under Section 15904.08.

To serve the protective purpose of Sections 15905.08 and 15905.09, in this subdivision "consent" must be understood as encompassing any form of approval, assent or acquiescence, whether formal or informal, express or tacit.

### California Code Comment
### By Phil Jelsma

Subsection (d)—The subdivision's limitation applies to the commencement of an action under subdivision (a) or (b) and not to subdivision (c), under which a general partner may implead other persons and is consistent with Corp Code Section 15666.

## ARTICLE 6.
## DISSOCIATION

## SECTION 15906.01. DISSOCIATION AS LIMITED PARTNER.

(a) A person does not have a right to dissociate as a limited partner before the termination of the limited partnership.

(b) A person is dissociated from a limited partnership as a limited partner upon the occurrence of any of the following events:

(1) the limited partnership's having notice of the person's express will to withdraw as a limited partner or on a later date specified by the person;

(2) an event agreed to in the partnership agreement as causing the person's dissociation as a limited partner;

(3) the person's expulsion as a limited partner pursuant to the partnership agreement;

(4) the person's expulsion as a limited partner by the unanimous consent of the other partners if:

(A) it is unlawful to carry on the limited partnership's activities with the person as a limited partner;

(B) there has been a transfer of all of the person's transferable interest in the limited partnership, other than a transfer for security purposes, or a court order charging the person's interest, which has not been foreclosed;

(C) the person is a corporation and, within 90 days after the limited partnership notifies the person that it will be expelled as a limited partner because it has filed a certificate of dissolution or the equivalent, its charter has been revoked, or its right to conduct business has been suspended by the jurisdiction of its incorporation, there is no revocation of the certificate of dissolution or no reinstatement of its charter or its right to conduct business; or

(D) the person is a limited liability company or partnership that has been dissolved and whose business is being wound up;

(5) on application by the limited partnership, the person's expulsion as a limited partner by judicial order because:

(A) the person engaged in wrongful conduct that adversely and materially affected the limited partnership's activities;

(B) the person willfully or persistently committed a material breach of the partnership agreement or of the obligation of good faith and fair dealing under subdivision (b) of Section 15903.05; or

(C) the person engaged in conduct relating to the limited partnership's activities which makes it not reasonably practicable to carry on the activities with the person as limited partner;

(6) in the case of a person who is an individual, the person's death;

(7) in the case of a person that is a trust or is acting as a limited partner by virtue of being a trustee of a trust, distribution of the trust's entire transferable interest in the limited partnership, but not merely by reason of the substitution of a successor trustee;

(8) in the case of a person that is an estate or is acting as a limited partner by virtue of being a personal representative of an estate, distribution of the estate's entire transferable interest in the limited partnership, but not merely by reason of the substitution of a successor personal representative;

(9) termination of a limited partner that is not an individual, partnership, limited liability company, corporation, trust, or estate;

(10) the limited partnership's participation in a conversion or merger under Article 11 (commencing with Section 15911.01), if the limited partnership:

(A) is not the converted or surviving entity; or

(B) is the converted or surviving entity but, as a result of the conversion or merger, the person ceases to be a limited partner.

## Uniform Limited Partnership Act Comment

Source—RUPA Section 601.

This section adopts RUPA's dissociation provision essentially verbatim, except for provisions inappropriate to limited partners. For example, this section does not provide for the dissociation of a person as a limited partner on account of bankruptcy, insolvency or incompetency.

This chapter refers to a person's dissociation as a limited partner rather than to the dissociation of a limited partner, because the same person may be both a general and a limited partner. See Section 15901.13 (Dual Capacity). It is possible for a dual capacity partner to dissociate in one capacity and not in the other.

**Subsection (a)**—This section varies substantially from predecessor law. See Comment to Section 15905.05.

**Subsection (b)(1)**—This provision gives a person the power to dissociate as a limited partner even though the dissociation is wrongful under subdivision (a). See, however, Section 15901.10(b)(8) (prohibiting the partnership agreement from eliminating the power of a person to dissociate as a general partner but imposing no comparable restriction with regard to a person's dissociation as a limited partner).

**Subsection (b)(5)**—In contrast to RUPA, this provision may be varied or even eliminated by the partnership agreement.

## SECTION 15906.02. EFFECT OF DISSOCIATION AS LIMITED PARTNER.

(a) Upon a person's dissociation as a limited partner:

(1) subject to Section 15907.04, the person does not have further rights as a limited partner;

(2) the person's obligation of good faith and fair dealing as a limited partner under subdivision(b) of Section 15903.05 continues only as to matters arising and events occurring before the dissociation; and

(3) subject to Section 15907.04 and Article 11 (commencing with Section 15911.01), any transferable interest owned by the person in the person's capacity as a limited partner immediately before dissociation is owned by the person as a mere transferee.

(b) A person's dissociation as a limited partner does not of itself discharge the person from any obligation to the limited partnership or the other partners which the person incurred while a limited partner.

### Uniform Limited Partnership Act Comment

**Source**—RUPA Section 603(b).

**Subsection (a)(1)**—In general, when a person dissociates as a limited partner, the person's rights as a limited partner disappear and, subject to Section 15901.13 (Dual Status), the person's status degrades to that of a mere transferee. However, Section 15907.04 provides some special rights when dissociation is caused by an individual's death.

**Subsection (a)(3)**—For any person that is both a general partner and a limited partner, the required records must state which transferable interest is owned in which capacity. Section 15901.11(8)(C).

Article 11 provides for conversions and mergers. A plan of conversion or merger may provide for the dissociation of a person as a limited partner and may override the rule stated in this paragraph.

## SECTION 15906.03. DISSOCIATION AS GENERAL PART-NER. A person is dissociated from a limited partnership as a general partner upon the occurrence of any of the following events:

(a) the limited partnership's having notice of the person's express will to withdraw as a general partner or on a later date specified by the person;

(b) an event agreed to in the partnership agreement as causing the persons dissociation as a general partner;

(c) the person's expulsion as a general partner pursuant to the partnership agreement;

(d) the person's expulsion as a general partner by the unanimous consent of the other partners if:

(1) it is unlawful to carry on the limited partnership's activities with the person as a general partner;

(2) there has been a transfer of all or substantially all of the person's transferable interest in the limited partnership, other than a transfer for security purposes, or a court order charging the person's interest, which has not been foreclosed;

(3) the person is a corporation and, within 90 days after the limited partnership notifies the person that it will be expelled as a general partner because it has filed a certificate of dissolution or the equivalent, its charter has been revoked, or its right to conduct business has been suspended by the jurisdiction of its incorporation, there is no revocation of the certificate of dissolution or no reinstatement of its charter or its right to conduct business; or

(4) the person is a limited liability company or partnership that has been dissolved and whose business is being wound up;

(e) on application by the limited partnership, the person's expulsion as a general partner by judicial order because:

(1) the person engaged in wrongful conduct that adversely and materially affected the limited partnership activities;

(2) the person willfully or persistently committed a material breach of the partnership agreement or of a duty owed to the partnership or the other partners under Section 15904.08; or

(3) the person engaged in conduct relating to the limited partnership's activities which makes it not reasonably practicable to carry on the activities of the limited partnership with the person as a general partner;

(f) the person's:

(1) becoming a debtor in bankruptcy;

(2) execution of an assignment for the benefit of creditors;

(3) seeking, consenting to, or acquiescing in the appointment of a trustee, receiver, or liquidator of the person or of all or substantially all of the person's property; or

(4) failure, within 90 days after the appointment, to have vacated or stayed the appointment of a trustee, receiver, or liquidator of the general partner or of all or substantially all of the person's property obtained without the person's consent or acquiescence, or failing within 90 days after the expiration of a stay to have the appointment vacated;

(g) in the case of a person who is an individual:

(1) the person's death;

(2) the appointment of a guardian or general conservator for the person; or

(3) a judicial determination that the person has otherwise become incapable of performing the person's duties as a general partner under the partnership agreement;

(h) in the case of a person that is a trust or is acting as a general partner by virtue of being a trustee of a trust, distribution of the trust's entire transferable interest in the limited partnership, but not merely by reason of the substitution of a successor trustee;

(i) in the case of a person that is an estate or is acting as a general partner by virtue of being a personal representative of an estate, distribution of the estate's entire transferable interest in the limited partnership, but not merely by reason of the substitution of a successor personal representative;

(j) termination of a general partner that is not an individual, partnership, limited liability company, corporation, trust, or estate; or

(k) the limited partnership's participation in a conversion or merger under Article 11 (commencing with Section 15911.01), if the limited partnership:

(1) is not the converted or surviving entity; or

(2) is the converted or surviving entity but, as a result of the conversion or merger, the person ceases to be a general partner.

## Uniform Limited Partnership Act Comment

**Source**—RUPA Section 601.

This section adopts RUPA's dissociation provision essentially verbatim. This chapter refers to a person's dissociation as a general partner rather than to the dissociation of a general partner, because the same person may be both a general and a limited partner. See Section 15901.13 (Dual Capacity). It is possible for a dual capacity partner to dissociate in one capacity and not in the other.

**Paragraph (1)**—The partnership agreement may not eliminate this power to dissociate. See Section 15901.10(b)(8).

**Paragraph (5)**—In contrast to RUPA, this provision may be varied or even eliminated by the partnership agreement.

## SECTION 15906.04. PERSON'S POWER TO DISSOCIATE AS GENERAL PARTNER; WRONGFUL DISSOCIATION.

(a) A person has the power to dissociate as a general partner at any time, rightfully or wrongfully, by express will pursuant to subdivision (a) of Section 15906.03.

(b) A person's dissociation as a general partner is wrongful only if:

(1) it is in breach of an express provision of the partnership agreement; or

(2) it occurs before the termination of the limited partnership, and:

(A) the person withdraws as a general partner by express will;

(B) the person is expelled as a general partner by judicial determination under subdivision (e) of Section 15906.03;

(C) the person is dissociated as a general partner by becoming a debtor in bankruptcy; or

(D) in the case of a person that is not an individual, trust other than a business trust, or estate, the person is expelled or otherwise dissociated as a general partner because it willfully dissolved or terminated.

(c) A person that wrongfully dissociates as a general partner is liable to the limited partnership and, subject to Section 15910.01, to the other partners for damages caused by the dissociation. The liability is in addition to any other obligation of the general partner to the limited partnership or to the other partners.

### Uniform Limited Partnership Act Comment

**Source**—RUPA Section 602.

**Subsection (a)**—The partnership agreement may not eliminate this power. See Section 15901.10(b)(8).

**Subsection (b)(1)**—The reference to "an express provision of the partnership agreement" means that a person's dissociation as a general partner in breach of the obligation of good faith and fair dealing is not wrongful dissociation for the purposes of this section. The breach might be actionable on other grounds.

**Subsection (b)(2)**—The reference to "before the termination of the limited partnership" reflects the expectation that each general partner will shepherd the limited partnership through winding up. See Comment to Section 15904.06(f). A person's obligation to remain as general partner through winding up continues even if another general partner dissociates and even if that dissociation leads to the limited partnership's premature dissolution under Section 15908.01(c)(1).

**Subsection (c)**—The language "subject to Section 15910.01" is intended to preserve the distinction between direct and derivative claims.

## SECTION 15906.05. EFFECT OF DISSOCIATION AS GENERAL PARTNER.

(a) Upon a person's dissociation as a general partner:

(1) the person's right to participate as a general partner in the management and conduct of the partnership's activities terminates;

(2) the person's duty of loyalty as a general partner under paragraph (3) of subdivision (b) of Section 15904.08 terminates;

(3) the person's duty of loyalty as a general partner under paragraphs (1) and (2) of subdivision (b) of Section 15904.08 and duty of care under subdivision (c) of Section 15904.08 continue only with regard to matters arising and events occurring before the person's dissociation as a general partner;

(4) the person may sign and deliver to the Secretary of State for filing, on a form prescribed by the Secretary of State, a certificate of dissociation pertaining to the person and, at the request of the limited partnership, shall sign an amendment to the certificate of limited partnership which states that the person has dissociated; and

(5) subject to Section 15907.04 and Article 11 (commencing with Section 15911.01), any transferable interest owned by the person immediately before dissociation in the person's capacity as a general partner is owned by the person as a mere transferee.

(b) A person's dissociation as a general partner does not of itself discharge the person from any obligation to the limited partnership or the other partners which the person incurred while a general partner.

### Uniform Limited Partnership Act Comment

**Source**—RUPA Section 603(b).

**Subsection (a)(1)**—Once a person dissociates as a general partner, the person loses all management rights as a general partner regardless of what happens to the limited partnership. This rule contrasts with RUPA Section 603(b)(1), which permits a dissociated general partner to participate in winding up in some circumstances.

**Subsection (a)(4)**—Both records covered by this paragraph have the same effect under Section 15901.03(d)—namely, to give constructive notice that the person has dissociated as a general partner. The notice benefits the person by curtailing any further personal liability under Sections 15906.07 and 15908.05. The notice benefits the limited partnership by curtailing any lingering power to bind under Sections 15906.06 and 15908.04.

The limited partnership is in any event obligated to amend its certificate of limited partnership to reflect the dissociation of a person as general partner. See Section 15902.02(b)(2). In most circumstances, the amendment requires the signature of the person that has dissociated. Section 15902.04(a)(5)(C). If that signature is required and the person refuses or fails to sign, the limited partnership may invoke Section 15902.05 (Signing and Filing Pursuant to Judicial Order).

**Subsection (a)(5)**—In general, when a person dissociates as a general partner, the person's rights as a general partner disappear and, subject to Section 15901.13 (Dual Status), the person's status degrades to that of a mere transferee. For any person that is both a general partner and a limited partner, the required records must state which transferable interest is owned in which capacity. Section 15901.11(8)(C).

**Section 15907.04** provides some special rights when an individual dissociates by dying. Article 11 provides for conversions and mergers. A plan of conversion or merger may provide for the dissociation of a person as a general partner and may override the rule stated in this paragraph.

## SECTION 15906.06. POWER TO BIND AND LIABILITY TO LIMITED PARTNERSHIP BEFORE DISSOLUTION OF PARTNERSHIP OF PERSON DISSOCIATED AS GENERAL PARTNER.

(a) After a person is dissociated as a general partner and before the limited partnership is dissolved, converted under Article 11 (commencing with Section 15911.01), or merged out of existence under that article, the limited partnership is bound by an act of the person only if:

(1) the act would have bound the limited partnership under Section 15904.02 before the dissociation; and

(2) at the time the other party enters into the transaction:

(A) less than two years have passed since the dissociation; and

(B) the other party does not have notice of the dissociation and reasonably believes that the person is a general partner.

(b) If a limited partnership is bound under subdivision (a), the person dissociated as a general partner which caused the limited partnership to be bound is liable:

(1) to the limited partnership for any damage caused to the limited partnership arising from the obligation incurred under subdivision (a); and

(2) if a general partner or another person dissociated as a general

partner is liable for the obligation, to the general partner or other person for any damage caused to the general partner or other person arising from the liability.

## Uniform Limited Partnership Act Comment

**Source**—RUPA Section 702.

This chapter contains two sections pertaining to the lingering power to bind of a person dissociated as a general partner:

this section, which applies until the limited partnership dissolves, converts to another form of organization under Article 11, or is merged out of existence under Article 11; and

Section 15908.04(b), which applies after a limited partnership dissolves.

**Subsection (a)(2)(B)**—A person might have notice under Section 15901.03(d)(1) as well as under Section 15901.03(b).

**Subsection (b)**—The liability provided by this subdivision is not exhaustive. For example, if a person dissociated as a general partner causes a limited partnership to be bound under subdivision (a) and, due to a guaranty, some other person is liable on the resulting obligation, that other person may have a claim under other law against the person dissociated as a general partner.

## SECTION 15906.07. LIABILITY TO OTHER PERSONS OF PERSON DISSOCIATED AS GENERAL PARTNER.

(a) A person's dissociation as a general partner does not of itself discharge the person's liability as a general partner for an obligation of the limited partnership incurred before dissociation. Except as otherwise provided in subdivisions (b) and (c), the person is not liable for a limited partnership's obligation incurred after dissociation.

(b) A person whose dissociation as a general partner resulted in a dissolution and winding up of the limited partnership's activities is liable to the same extent as a general partner under Section 15904.04 on an obligation incurred by the limited partnership under Section 15908.04.

(c) A person that has dissociated as a general partner but whose dissociation did not result in a dissolution and winding up of the limited partnership's activities is liable on a transaction entered into by the limited partnership after the dissociation only if:

(1) a general partner would be liable on the transaction; and

(2) at the time the other party enters into the transaction:

(A) less than two years have passed since the dissociation; and

(B) the other party does not have notice of the dissociation and reasonably believes that the person is a general partner.

(d) By agreement with a creditor of a limited partnership and the limited partnership, a person dissociated as a general partner may be released from liability to the creditor for an obligation of the limited partnership.

(e) A person dissociated as a general partner is released from liability for an obligation of the limited partnership if the limited partnership's creditor, with notice of the person's dissociation as a general partner but without the person's consent, agrees to a material alteration in the nature or time of payment of the obligation.

## Uniform Limited Partnership Act Comment

**Source**—RUPA Section 703.

A person's dissociation as a general partner does not categorically prevent the person from being liable as a general partner for subsequently incurred obligations of the limited partnership. If the dissociation results in dissolution, subdivision (b) applies and the person will be liable as a general partner on any partnership obligation incurred under Section 15908.04. In these circumstances, neither filing a statement of dissociation nor amending the certificate of limited partnership to state that the person has dissociated as a general partner will curtail the person's lingering exposure to liability.

If the dissociation does not result in dissolution, subdivision (c) applies. In this context, filing a statement of dissociation or amending the certificate of limited partnership to state that the person has dissociated as a general partner will curtail the person's lingering liability. See subdivision (c)(2)(B).

If the limited partnership subsequently dissolves as the result of some other occurrence (*i.e.,* not a result of the person's dissociation as a general partner), subdivision (c) continues to apply. In that situation, Section 15908.04 will determine whether, for the purposes of subdivision (c), the limited partnership has entered into a transaction after dissolution.

**Subsection (a)**—The phrase "liability as a general partner for an obligation of the limited partnership" refers to liability under Section 15904.04. Following RUPA and the UPA, this chapter leaves to other law the question of when a limited partnership obligation is incurred.

## ARTICLE 7.
## TRANSFERABLE INTERESTS AND RIGHTS
## OF TRANSFEREES AND CREDITORS

**SECTION 15907.01. PARTNER'S TRANSFERABLE INTEREST.** The only interest of a partner which is transferable is the partner's transferable interest. A transferable interest is personal property.

## Uniform Limited Partnership Act Comment

**Source**—RUPA Section 502.

Like all other partnership statutes, this chapter dichotomizes each partner's rights into economic rights and other rights. The former are freely transferable, as provided in Section 15907.02. The latter are not transferable at all, unless the partnership agreement so provides.

Although a partner or transferee owns a transferable interest as a present right, that right only entitles the owner to distributions if and when made. See Sections 15904.05 (subject to any contrary provision in the partnership agreement, no right to interim distribution unless the limited partnership decides to make an interim distribution) and the Comment to Section 15908.09 (subject to any contrary provision in the partnership agreement, no partner obligated to contribute for the purpose of equalizing or otherwise allocating capital losses).

## SECTION 15907.02. TRANSFER OF PARTNER'S TRANS-FERABLE INTEREST.

(a) A transfer, in whole or in part, of a partner's transferable interest:

(1) is permissible;

(2) does not by itself cause the partner's dissociation or a dissolution and winding up of the limited partnership's activities; and

(3) does not, as against the other partners or the limited partnership, entitle the transferee to participate in the management or conduct of the limited partnership's activities, to require access to information concerning the limited partnership's transactions except as otherwise provided in subdivision (c), or to inspect or copy the required information or the limited partnership's other records or to exercise any other rights or powers of a partner.

(b) A transferee has a right to receive, in accordance with the transfer,

distributions to which the transferor would otherwise be entitled.

(c) A transferee is entitled to an account of the limited partnership's transactions only upon the dissolution and winding up of the limited partnership.

(d) Upon transfer, the transferor retains the rights of a partner other than the interest in distributions transferred and retains all duties and obligations of a partner.

(e) A limited partnership need not give effect to a transferee's rights under this section until the limited partnership has notice of the transfer.

(f) A transfer of a partner's transferable interest in the limited partnership in violation of a restriction on transfer contained in the partnership agreement is ineffective as to a person having notice of the restriction at the time of transfer.

(g) A transferee that becomes a partner with respect to a transferable interest is liable for the transferor's obligations under Sections 15905.02 and 15905.09. However, the transferee is not obligated for liabilities unknown to the transferee at the time the transferee became a partner.

(h) A transferee of a partnership interest, including a transferee of a general partner, may become a limited partner if, and to the extent that (1) the partnership agreement provides or (2) all general partners and a majority in interest of the limited partners consent.

### Uniform Limited Partnership Act Comment

**Source**—RUPA Section 503, except for subdivision (g), which derives from RULPA Section 704(b). Following RUPA, this chapter uses the words "transfer" and "transferee" rather than the words "assignment" and "assignee." See RUPA Section 503.

**Subsection (a)(2)**—The phrase "by itself" is significant. A transfer of all of a person's transferable interest could lead to dissociation via expulsion, Sections 15906.01(b)(4)(B) and 15906.03(d)(2).

**Subsection (a)(3)**—Mere transferees have no right to intrude as the partners carry on their activities as partners. Moreover, a partner's obligation of good faith and fair dealing under Sections 15903.05(b) and 15904.08(d) is framed in reference to "the limited partnership and the other partners."

## SECTION 15907.03. RIGHTS OF CREDITOR OF PARTNER OR TRANSFEREE.

(a) On application to a court of competent jurisdiction by any judgment creditor of a partner or transferee, the court may charge the transferable interest of the judgment debtor with payment of the unsatisfied amount of the judgment with interest. To the extent so charged, the judgment creditor has only the rights of a transferee. The court may appoint a receiver of the share of the distributions due or to become due to the judgment debtor in respect of the limited partnership and make all other orders, directions, accounts, and inquiries the judgment debtor might have made or which the circumstances of the case may require to give effect to the charging order.

(b) A charging order constitutes a lien on the judgment debtor's transferable interest. The court may order a foreclosure upon the interest subject to the charging order at any time. The purchaser at the foreclosure sale has the rights of a transferee.

(c) At any time before foreclosure, an interest charged may be redeemed:

(1) by the judgment debtor;

(2) with property other than limited partnership property, by one or more of the other partners; or

(3) with limited partnership property, by the limited partnership with the consent of all partners whose interests are not so charged.

(d) This chapter does not deprive any partner or transferee of the benefit of any exemption laws applicable to the partner's or transferee's transferable interest.

(e) This section provides the exclusive remedy by which a judgment creditor of a partner or transferee may satisfy a judgment out of the judgment debtor's transferable interest.

(f) No creditor of a partner shall have any right to obtain possession or otherwise exercise legal or equitable remedies with respect to the property of the limited partnership.

## Uniform Limited Partnership Act Comment

**Source**—RUPA Section 504 and ULLCA Section 504.

This section balances the needs of a judgment creditor of a partner or transferee with the needs of the limited partnership and non-debtor partners and transferees. The section achieves that balance by allowing the judgment creditor to collect on the judgment through the transferable interest of the judgment debtor while prohibiting interference in the management and activities of the limited partnership.

Under this section, the judgment creditor of a partner or transferee is entitled to a charging order against the relevant transferable interest. While in effect, that order entitles the judgment creditor to whatever distributions would otherwise be due to the partner or transferee whose interest is subject to the order. The creditor has no say in the timing or amount of those distributions. The charging order does not entitle the creditor to accelerate any distributions or to otherwise interfere with the management and activities of the limited partnership.

Foreclosure of a charging order effects a permanent transfer of the charged transferable interest to the purchaser. The foreclosure does not, however, create any rights to participate in the management and conduct of the limited partnership's activities. The purchaser obtains nothing more than the status of a transferee.

**Subsection (a)**—The court's power to appoint a receiver and "make all other orders, directions, accounts, and inquiries the judgment debtor might have made or which the circumstances of the case may require" must be understood in the context of the balance described above. In particular, the court's power to make orders "which the circumstances may require" is limited to "giv[ing] effect to the charging order."

Example: A judgment creditor with a charging order believes that the limited partnership should invest less of its surplus in operations, leaving more funds for distributions. The creditor moves the court for an order directing the general partners to restrict re-investment. This section does not authorize the court to grant the motion.

Example: A judgment creditor with a judgment for $10,000 against a partner obtains a charging order against the partner's transferable interest. The limited partnership is duly served with the order. However, the limited partnership subsequently fails to comply with the order and makes a $3,000 distribution to the partner. The court has the power to order the limited partnership to turn over $3000 to the judgment creditor to "give effect to the charging order."

The court also has the power to decide whether a particular payment is a distribution, because this decision determines whether the payment is part of a transferable interest subject to a charging order. (To the extent a payment is not a distribution, it is not part of the transferable interest and is not subject to subdivision (e). The payment is therefore subject to whatever other creditor remedies may apply.)

**Subsection (c)(3)**—This provision requires the consent of all the limited as well as general partners.

## SECTION 15907.04. POWER OF ESTATE OF DECEASED PARTNER. If a partner dies, the deceased partner's personal representative or other legal representative may exercise the rights of a transferee as provided in Section 15907.02 and, for the purposes of settling the estate, may exercise the rights of a current limited partner under Section 15903.04.

### Uniform Limited Partnership Act Comment

Section 15907.02 strictly limits the rights of transferees. In particular, a transferee has no right to participate in management in any way, no voting rights and, except following dissolution, no information rights. Even after dissolution, a transferee's information rights are limited. See Section 15907.02(c).This section provides special informational rights for a deceased partner's legal representative for the purposes of settling the estate. For those purposes, the legal representative may exercise the informational rights of a current limited partner under Section 15903.04. Those rights are of course subject to the limitations and obligations stated in that section—*e.g.,* Section 15903.04(g) (restrictions on use) and (h) (charges for copies)—as well as any generally applicable limitations stated in the partnership agreement.

## ARTICLE 8.
## DISSOLUTION

## SECTION 15908.01. NONJUDICIAL DISSOLUTION. Except as otherwise provided in Section 15908.02, a limited partnership is dissolved, and its activities must be wound up, only upon the occurrence of any of the following:

(a) the happening of an event specified in the partnership agreement;

(b) the consent of all general partners and of limited partners owning a majority of the rights to receive distributions as limited partners at the time the consent is to be effective;

(c) after the dissociation of a person as a general partner:

(1) if the limited partnership has at least one remaining general partner, and a consent to dissolve the limited partnership is given within 90 days after the dissociation by partners owning a majority of the rights to receive distributions as partners at the time the consent is to be effective; or

(2) if the limited partnership does not have a remaining general partner, the passage of 90 days after the dissociation, unless before the end of the period:

(A) consent to continue the activities of the limited partnership and admit at least one general partner is given by limited partners owning a majority of the rights to receive distributions as limited partners at the time the consent is to be effective; and

(B) at least one person is admitted as a general partner in accordance with the consent; or

(C) the passage of 90 days after the dissociation of the limited partnership's last limited partner, unless before the end of the period the limited partnership admits at least one limited partner.

## Uniform Limited Partnership Act Comment

This chapter does not require that any of the consents referred to in this section be given in the form of a signed record. The partnership agreement has the power to impose that requirement. See Comment to Section 15901.10.

In several provisions, this section provides for consent in terms of rights to receive distributions. Distribution rights of non-partner transferees are not relevant. Mere transferees have no consent rights, and their distribution rights are not counted in determining whether majority consent has been obtained.

**Paragraph (1)**—There is no requirement that the relevant provision of the partnership agreement be made in a record, unless the partnership agreement creates that requirement. However, if the relevant provision is not "contained in a partnership agreement made in a record," Section 15901.11(8)(D) includes among the limited partnership's required information "a record stating . . . any events upon the happening of which the limited partnership is to be dissolved and its activities wound up."

**Paragraph (2)**—Rights to receive distributions owned by a person that is both a general and a limited partner figure into the limited partner determination only to the extent those rights are owned in the person's capacity as a limited partner. See Section 15901.11(8)(C).

Example: XYZ is a limited partnership with three general partners, each of whom is also a limited partner, and 5 other limited partners. Rights to receive distributions are allocated as follows:

* partner #1 as general partner—3%

* partner #2 as general partner—2%

* partner #3 as general partner—1%

* partner #1 as limited partner—7%

* partner #2 as limited partner—3%

* partner #3 as limited partner—4%

* partner #4 as limited partner—5%

* partner #5 as limited partner—5%

* partner #6 as limited partner—5%

* partner #7 as limited partner—5%

* partner #8 as limited partner—5%

* Several non-partner transferees, in the aggregate—55%

Distribution rights owned by persons as limited partners amount to 39% of total distribution rights. A majority is therefore anything greater than 19.5%. If only partners 1, 2, 3 and 4 consent to dissolve, the limited partnership is not dissolved. Together these partners own as limited partners 19% of the distribution rights owned by persons as limited partners—just short of the necessary majority. For purposes of this calculation, distribution rights owned by non-partner transferees are irrelevant. So, too, are distribution rights owned by persons as general partners. (However, dissolution under this provision requires "the consent of all general partners.")

**Paragraph (3)(A)**—Unlike paragraph (2), this paragraph makes no distinction between distribution rights owned by persons as general partners and distribution rights owned by persons as limited partners. Distribution rights owned by non-partner transferees are irrelevant.

## SECTION 15908.02. JUDICIAL DISSOLUTION.

(a) On application by a partner, a court of competent jurisdiction may order dissolution of a limited partnership if it is not reasonably practicable to carry on the activities of the limited partnership in conformity with the partnership agreement.

(b) In any suit for judicial dissolution, the other partners may avoid the dissolution of the limited partnership by purchasing for cash the partnership interests owned by the partners so initiating the proceeding (the "moving parties") at their fair market value.

In fixing the value, the amount of any damages resulting if the initiation of the dissolution is a breach by any moving party or parties of an agreement with the purchasing party or parties, including, without limitation, the partnership agreement, may be deducted from the amount payable to the moving party or parties.

(c) If the purchasing parties (1) elect to purchase the partnership interests owned by the moving parties, (2) are unable to agree with the moving parties upon the fair market value of the partnership interests, and (3) give bond with sufficient security to pay the estimated reasonable expenses, including attorneys' fees, of the moving parties if the expenses are recoverable under paragraph (3), the court, upon application of the purchasing parties, either in the pending action or in a proceeding initiated in the superior court of the proper county by the purchasing parties, shall stay the winding up and dissolution proceeding and shall proceed to ascertain and fix the fair market value of the partnership interests owned by the moving parties.

(d) The court shall appoint three disinterested appraisers to appraise the fair market value of the partnership interests owned by the moving parties, and shall make an order referring the matter to the appraisers so appointed for the purpose of ascertaining that value. The order shall prescribe the time and manner of producing evidence, if evidence is required. The award of the appraisers or a majority of them, when confirmed by the court, shall be final and conclusive upon all parties. The court shall enter a decree that shall provide in the alternative for winding up and dissolution of the limited partnership unless payment is made for the partnership interests within the time specified by the decree. If the purchasing parties do not make payment for the partnership interests within the time specified, judgment shall be entered against them and the surety or sureties on the bond for the amount of the expenses, including attorneys' fees, of the moving parties. Any member aggrieved by the action of the court may' appeal therefrom.

(e) If the purchasing parties desire to prevent the winding up and dissolution of the limited partnership, they shall pay to the moving parties the value of their partnership interests ascertained and decreed within the time specified pursuant to this section, or, in the case of an appeal, as fixed on appeal. On receiving that payment or the tender thereof, the moving parties shall transfer their partnership interests to the purchasing parties.

(f) For the purposes of this section, the valuation date shall be the date upon which the action for judicial dissolution was commenced. However, the court may, upon the hearing of a motion by any party, and for good cause shown, designate some other date as the valuation date.

### Uniform Limited Partnership Act Comment

**Source**—RULPA Section 802.

**Section 15901.10(b)(9)** limits the power of the partnership agreement with regard to this section.

### California Code Comment
### By Phil Jelsma

**Source**—Sections 15908.02(b)–(g) from Cal. Corp. Code Section 17351.

## SECTION 15908.03. WINDING UP.

(a) A limited partnership continues after dissolution only for the purpose of winding up its activities.

(b) In winding up its activities, the limited partnership:

(1) may amend its certificate of limited partnership to state that the limited partnership is dissolved, preserve the limited partnership business or property as a going concern for a reasonable time, prosecute and defend actions and proceedings, whether civil, criminal, or administrative, transfer the limited partnership's property, settle disputes by mediation or arbitration, file a certificate of cancellation as provided in Section 15902.03, and perform other necessary acts; and

(2) shall discharge the limited partnership's liabilities, settle and close the limited partnership's activities, and marshal and distribute the assets of the partnership.

(c) If a dissolved limited partnership does not have a general partner, a person to wind up the dissolved limited partnership's activities may be appointed by the consent of limited partners owning a majority of the rights to receive distributions as limited partners at the time the consent is to be effective. A person appointed under this subdivision:

(1) has the powers of a general partner under Section 15908.04; and

(2) shall promptly amend the certificate of limited partnership to state:

(A) that the limited partnership does not have a general partner;

(B) the name of the person that has been appointed to wind up the limited partnership; and

(C) the address of the person.

(d) On the application of any partner, the appropriate court may order judicial supervision of the winding up, including the appointment of a person to wind up the dissolved limited partnership's activities, if:

(1) a limited partnership does not have a general partner and within a reasonable time following the dissolution no person has been appointed pursuant to subdivision (c); or

(2) the applicant establishes other good cause.

(e) Unless otherwise provided in the partnership agreement, the limited partners winding up the affairs of the partnership pursuant to this section shall be entitled to reasonable compensation.

### Uniform Limited Partnership Act Comment

**Source**—RUPA Sections 802 and 803.

**Subsection (b)(2)**—A limited partnership may satisfy its duty to "discharge" a liability either by paying or by making an alternative arrangement satisfactory to the creditor.

**Subsection (c)**—The method for determining majority consent is analogous to the method applicable under Section 15908.01(b). See the Comment to that paragraph.

A person appointed under this subdivision is not a general partner and therefore is not subject to Section 15904.08.

### SECTION 15908.04. POWER OF GENERAL PARTNER AND PERSON DISSOCIATED AS GENERAL PARTNER TO BIND PARTNERSHIP AFTER DISSOLUTION.

(a) A limited partnership is bound by a general partner's act after dissolution which:

(1) is appropriate for winding up the limited partnership's activities; or

(2) would have bound the limited partnership under Section 15904.02 before dissolution, if, at the time the other party enters into the transaction, the other party does not have notice of the dissolution.

(b) A person dissociated as a general partner binds a limited partnership through an act occurring after dissolution if:

(1) at the time the other party enters into the transaction:

(A) less than two years have passed since the dissociation; and

(B) the other party does not have notice of the dissociation and reasonably believes that the person is a general partner; and

(2) the act:

(A) is appropriate for winding up the limited partnership's activities; or

(B) would have bound the limited partnership under Section 15904.02 before dissolution and at the time the other party enters into the transaction the other party does not have notice of the dissolution.

### Uniform Limited Partnership Act Comment

**Subsection (a)**—Source: RUPA Section 804.

**Subsection (a)(2)**—A person might have notice under Section 15901.03(d)(2) (amendment of certificate of limited partnership to indicate dissolution) as well as under Section 15901.03(b).

**Subsection (b)**—This subdivision deals with the post-dissolution power to bind of a person dissociated as a general partner. Paragraph (1) replicates the provisions of Section 15906.06, pertaining to the pre-dissolution power to bind of a person dissociated as a general partner. Paragraph (2) replicates the provisions of subdivision (a), which state the post-dissolution power to bind of a general partner. For a person dissociated as a general partner to bind a dissolved limited partnership, the person's act will have to satisfy both paragraph (1) and paragraph (2).

**Subsection (b)(1)(B)**—A person might have notice under Section 15901.03(d)(1) as well as under Section 15901.03(b).

**Subsection (b)(2)(B)**—A person might have notice under Section 15901.03(d)(2) (amendment of certificate of limited partnership to indicate dissolution) as well as under Section 15901.03(b).

## SECTION 15908.05. LIABILITY AFTER DISSOLUTION OF GENERAL PARTNER AND PERSON DISSOCIATED AS GENERAL PARTNER TO LIMITED PARTNERSHIP, OTHER GENERAL PARTNERS, AND PERSONS DISSOCIATED AS GENERAL PARTNER.

(a) If a general partner having knowledge of the dissolution causes a limited partnership to incur an obligation under subdivision (a) of Section 15908.04 by an act that is not appropriate for winding up the partnership's activities, the general partner is liable:

(1) to the limited partnership for any damage caused to the limited partnership arising from the obligation; and

(2) if another general partner or a person dissociated as a general partner is liable for the obligation, to that other general partner or person for any damage caused to that other general partner or person arising from the liability.

(b) If a person dissociated as a general partner causes a limited partnership to incur an obligation under subdivision (b) of Section 15908.04, the person is liable:

(1) to the limited partnership for any damage caused to the limited partnership arising from the obligation; and

(2) if a general partner or another person dissociated as a general partner is liable for the obligation, to the general partner or other person for any damage caused to the general partner or other person arising from the liability.

## Uniform Limited Partnership Act Comment

**Source**—RUPA Section 806.

It is possible for more than one person to be liable under this section on account of the same limited partnership obligation. This chapter does not provide any rule for apportioning liability in that circumstance.

**Subsection (a)(2)**—If the limited partnership is not a limited liability limited partnership, the liability created by this paragraph includes liability under Sections 15904.04(a), 15906.07(b), and 15906.07(c). The paragraph also applies when a partner or person dissociated as a general partner suffers damage due to a contract of guaranty.

## SECTION 15908.06. KNOWN CLAIMS AGAINST DISSOLVED LIMITED PARTNERSHIP.

(a) A dissolved limited partnership may dispose of the known claims against it by following the procedure described in subdivision (b).

(b) A dissolved limited partnership may notify its known claimants of the dissolution in a record. The notice must:

(1) specify the information required to be included in a claim;

(2) provide a mailing address to which the claim is to be sent;

(3) state the deadline for receipt of the claim, which may not be less than 120 days after the date the notice is received by the claimant; and

(4) state that the claim will be barred if not received by the deadline.

(c) A claim against a dissolved limited partnership is barred if the requirements of subdivision (b) are met and:

(1) the claim is not received by the specified deadline; or

(2) in the case of a claim that is timely received but rejected in writing by the dissolved limited partnership, the claimant does not commence an action to enforce the claim against the limited partnership within 90 days after the receipt of a written notice of the rejection.

(d) This section does not apply to a claim based on an event occurring after the effective date of dissolution or a liability that is contingent on that date.

### Uniform Limited Partnership Act Comment

Source—ULLCA Section 807. See also RMBCA Section 14.06.

### SECTION 15908.07. OTHER CLAIMS AGAINST DISSOLVED LIMITED PARTNERSHIP.

(a) A dissolved limited partnership may publish notice of its dissolution and request persons having claims against the limited partnership to present them in accordance with the notice.

(b) The notice must:

(1) be published at least once in a newspaper of general circulation in the county in which the dissolved limited partnership's principal office is located or, if it has none in this state, in the county in which the limited partnership's designated office is or was last located;

(2) describe the information required to be contained in a claim and provide a mailing address to which the claim is to be sent; and

(3) state that a claim against the limited partnership is barred unless an action to enforce the claim is commenced within four years after publication of the notice.

(c) If a dissolved limited partnership publishes a notice in accordance with subdivision (b), the claim of each of the following claimants is barred unless the claimant commences an action to enforce the claim against the dissolved limited partnership within four years after the publication date of the notice:

(1) a claimant that did not receive notice in a record under Section 15908.06;

(2) a claimant whose claim was timely sent to the dissolved limited partnership but not acted on; and

(3) a claimant whose claim is contingent or based on an event occurring after the effective date of dissolution.

(d) A claim not barred under this section may be enforced:

(1) against the dissolved limited partnership, to the extent of its undistributed assets;

(2) if the assets have been distributed in liquidation, against a partner or transferee to the extent of that person's proportionate share

of the claim or the limited partnership's assets distributed to the partner or transferee in liquidation, whichever is less, but a person's total liability for all claims under this paragraph does not exceed the total amount of assets distributed to the person as part of the winding up of the dissolved limited partnership; or

(3) against any person liable on the claim under Section 15904.04.

(e) Publication of a notice of dissolution of a limited partnership pursuant to this section shall not bar the collection of any tax, interest, penalty or addition to tax under Part 10 (commencing with Section 17001) of, Part 10.20 (commencing with Section 18401) of, and Part 11 (commencing with Section 23001) of, Division 2 of the Revenue and Taxation Code.

## Uniform Limited Partnership Act Comment

Source—**ULLCA Section 808. See also RMBCA Section 14.07.**

## SECTION 15908.08. LIABILITY OF GENERAL PARTNER AND PERSON DISSOCIATED AS GENERAL PARTNER WHEN CLAIM AGAINST LIMITED PARTNERSHIP BARRED. If a claim against a dissolved limited partnership is barred under Section 15908.06 or 15908.07, any corresponding claim under Section 15904.04 is also barred.

## Uniform Limited Partnership Act Comment

The liability under Section 15904.04 of a general partner or person dissociated as a general partner is merely liability for the obligations of the limited partnership.

## SECTION 15908.09. DISPOSITION OF ASSETS; WHEN CONTRIBUTIONS REQUIRED.

(a) In winding up a limited partnership's activities, the assets of the limited partnership, including the contributions required by this section, must be applied to satisfy the limited partnership's obligations to creditors, including, to the extent permitted by law, partners that are creditors.

(b) Any surplus remaining after the limited partnership complies with subdivision (a) must be returned to the partners as they share in distributions.

(c) If a limited partnership's assets are insufficient to satisfy all of its obligations under subdivision (a), the following rules apply:

(1) Each person that was a general partner when the obligation was incurred and that has not been released from the obligation

under Section 15906.07 shall contribute to the limited partnership for the purpose of enabling the limited partnership to satisfy the obligation. The contribution due from each of those persons is in proportion to the right to receive distributions in the capacity of general partner in effect for each of those persons when the obligation was incurred.

(2) If a person does not contribute the full amount required under paragraph (1) with respect to an unsatisfied obligation of the limited partnership, the other persons required to contribute by paragraph (1) on account of the obligation shall contribute the additional amount necessary to discharge the obligation. The additional contribution due from each of those other persons is in proportion to the right to receive distributions in the capacity of general partner in effect for each of those other persons when the obligation was incurred.

(3) If a person does not make the additional contribution required by paragraph (2), further additional contributions are determined and due in the same manner as provided in that paragraph.

(d) A person that makes an additional contribution under paragraph (2) or (3) of subdivision (c) may recover from any person whose failure to contribute under paragraph (1) or (2) of subdivision (c) necessitated the additional contribution. A person may not recover under this subdivision more than the amount additionally contributed. A person's liability under this subdivision may not exceed the amount the person failed to contribute.

(e) The estate of a deceased individual is liable for the person's obligations under this section.

(f) An assignee for the benefit of creditors of a limited partnership or a partner, or a person appointed by a court to represent creditors of a limited partnership or a partner, may enforce a person's obligation to contribute under subdivision (c).

## Uniform Limited Partnership Act Comment

In some circumstances, this chapter requires a partner to make payments to the limited partnership. See, *e.g.*, Sections 15905.02(b), 15905.09(a), and 15905.09(b). In other circumstances, this chapter requires a partner to make payments to other partners. See, e.g., Section 15905.09(c). In no circumstances does this chapter require a partner to make a payment for the purpose of equalizing or otherwise reallocating capital losses incurred by partners.

Example: XYZ limited partnership ("XYZ") has one general partner and four limited partners. According to XYZ's required information, the value of each partner's contributions to XYZ are:

General partner—$5,000

Limited partner #1—$10,000

Limited partner #2—$15,000

Limited partner #3—$20,000

Limited partner #4—$25,000

XYZ is unsuccessful and eventually dissolves without ever having made a distribution to its partners. XYZ lacks any assets with which to return to the partners the value of their respective contributions. No partner is obliged to make any payment either to the limited partnership or to fellow partners to adjust these capital losses. These losses are not part of "the limited partnership's obligations to creditors." Section 15908.09(a).

Example: Same facts, except that Limited Partner #4 loaned $25,000 to XYZ when XYZ was not a limited liability limited partnership, and XYZ lacks the assets to repay the loan. The general partner must contribute to the limited partnership whatever funds are necessary to enable XYZ to satisfy the obligation owned to Limited Partner #4 on account of the loan. Section 15908.09(a) and (c).

**Subsection (c)**—Following RUPA and the UPA, this chapter leaves to other law the question of when a limited partnership obligation is incurred.

## ARTICLE 9.
## FOREIGN LIMITED PARTNERSHIPS

### SECTION 15909.01. GOVERNING LAW.

(a) The laws of the state or other jurisdiction under which a foreign limited partnership is organized govern relations among the partners of the foreign limited partnership and between the partners and the foreign limited partnership and the liability of partners as partners for an obligation of the foreign limited partnership except as to foreign limited liability limited partnerships which shall be treated as if they were foreign limited partnerships.

(b) A foreign limited partnership may not be denied a certificate of registration by reason of any difference between the laws of the jurisdiction under which the foreign limited partnership is organized and the laws of this state.

(c) A certificate of registration does not authorize a foreign limited partnership to engage in any business or exercise any power that a limited partnership may not engage in or exercise in this state.

### Uniform Limited Partnership Act Comment

**Source**—ULLCA Section 1001 for subdivisions (b) and (c).

**Subsection (a)**—This subdivision parallels and is analogous in scope and effect to Section 15901.06 (choice of law for domestic limited partnerships).

**Subsection (b)**—This subdivision prohibits denial of registration to a foreign limited liability partnership.

## SECTION 15909.02. APPLICATION FOR CERTIFICATE OF REGISTRATION.

(a) A foreign limited partnership may apply for a certificate of registration to transact business in this state by delivering an application signed and acknowledged by a general partner of the foreign limited partnership to and on a form prescribed by, the Secretary of State for filing. The application must state:

(1) the name of the foreign limited partnership and, if the name does not comply with Section 15901.08, an alternate name adopted pursuant to subdivision (a) of Section 15909.05

(2) the name of the state or other jurisdiction under whose law the foreign limited partnership is organized and the date of its formation;

(3) the address of the foreign limited partnership's designated office and, if the laws of the jurisdiction under which the foreign limited partnership is organized require the foreign limited partnership to maintain an office in that jurisdiction, the address of the required office;

(4) the name and address of the foreign limited partnership's initial agent for service of process in this state in accordance with paragraph (1) of subdivision (a) of Section 15901.16;

(5) the name and address of each of the foreign limited partnership's general partners; and

(6) whether the foreign limited partnership is a foreign limited liability limited partnership.

(b) A foreign limited partnership shall deliver with the completed application a certificate of existence or a record of similar import signed by the Secretary of State or other official having custody of the foreign limited partnership's publicly filed records in the state or other jurisdiction under whose law the foreign limited partnership is organized.

### Uniform Limited Partnership Act Comment

Source—ULLCA Section 1002.

## SECTION 15909.03. ACTIVITIES NOT CONSTITUTING TRANSACTING BUSINESS.

(a) Activities of a foreign limited partnership that do not constitute transacting business in this state for registration purposes within the meaning of this article include the activities set forth in subdivision (ai) of Section 15901.02.

(b) For purposes of this article, the ownership in this state of income-producing real property or tangible personal property, other than property excluded under subdivision (a), constitutes transacting business in this state.

(c) This section does not apply in determining the contacts or activities that may subject a foreign limited partnership to service of process, taxation, jurisdiction or regulation under any other law of this state.

### Uniform Limited Partnership Act Comment

Source—ULLCA Section 1003.

**SECTION 15909.04. FILING OF CERTIFICATE OF REGISTRATION.** Unless the Secretary of State determines that an application for a certificate of registration does not comply with the filing requirements of this chapter, the Secretary of State, upon payment of all requisite fees, shall file the application and shall issue to the foreign limited partnership a certificate of registration stating the date of filing of the application and that the foreign limited partnership is qualified to transact intrastate business, subject, however, to any licensing requirements otherwise imposed by the laws of this state.

### Uniform Limited Partnership Act Comment

Source—ULLCA Section 1004 and RULPA Section 903.

**SECTION 15909.05. NONCOMPLYING NAME OF FOREIGN LIMITED PARTNERSHIP.**

(a) A foreign limited partnership whose name does not comply with Section 15901.08 may not obtain a certificate of registration until it adopts, for the purpose of transacting business in this state, an alternate name that complies with Section 15901.08.

(b) If a foreign limited partnership authorized to transact business in this state changes its name to one that does not comply with Section 15901.08, it may not thereafter transact business in this state until it complies with subdivision (a) and obtains an amended certificate of registration.

(c) The Secretary of State may cancel the application and certificate of registration of a foreign limited partnership if a check or other remittance accepted in payment of the filing fee is not paid upon presentation. Upon receiving written notification that the item presented for payment has not been honored for payment, the Secretary of State shall give a first written notice of the applicability of this section to the agent for service of process or to the person submitting the instrument. Thereafter, if the amount has not been paid by cashier's check or equivalent, the Secretary of State shall give a second written notice of cancellation and the cancellation shall thereupon be effective. The second notice shall be given 20 days or more after the first notice and 90 days or less after the original filing.

### SECTION 15909.06 LIABILITY FOR FALSE STATEMENT.

If any statement in the application for registration of a foreign limited partnership was false when made or any statements made have become erroneous, the foreign limited partnership shall promptly deliver to, and on a form prescribed by the Secretary of State an amendment to the application for registration, signed and acknowledged by the general partner amending the statement.

#### Uniform Limited Partnership Act Comment

Source—ULLCA Section 1005.

### SECTION 15909.07. CANCELLATION OF CERTIFICATE OF REGISTRATION; EFFECT OF FAILURE TO HAVE CERTIFICATE.

(a) In order to cancel its certificate of registration to transact business in this state, a foreign limited partnership must deliver to and on a form prescribed by the Secretary of State for filing a certificate of cancellation signed and acknowledged by a general partner of the foreign limited partnership. The registration is canceled when the certificate becomes effective under Section 15902.06.

(b) A foreign limited partnership transacting business in this state may not maintain an action or proceeding in this state unless it has a certificate of registration to transact business in this state.

(c) Any foreign limited partnership that transacts intrastate business in this state without registration is subject to a penalty of twenty dollars ($20) for each day that the unauthorized intrastate business is transacted, up to a maximum of ten thousand dollars ($10,000). An action to recover this penalty may be brought, and any recovery shall be paid, as provided in Section 2258.

(d) The failure of a foreign limited partnership to have a certificate of registration to transact business in this state does not impair the validity of a contract or act of the foreign limited partnership or prevent the foreign limited partnership from defending an action or proceeding in this state.

(e) A partner of a foreign limited partnership is not liable for the obligations of the foreign limited partnership solely by reason of the foreign limited partnership's having transacted business in this state without a certificate of registration.

(f) If a foreign limited partnership transacts business in this state without a certificate of registration or cancels its certificate of registration, it appoints the Secretary of State as its agent for service of process for rights of action arising out of the transaction of business in this state.

### Uniform Limited Partnership Act Comment

Source—RULPA Section 907(d); ULLCA Section 1008.

## SECTION 15909.08. ACTION BY ATTORNEY GENERAL.
The Attorney General may maintain an action to restrain a foreign limited partnership from transacting business in this state in violation of this article.

### Uniform Limited Partnership Act Comment

Source—RULPA Section 908; ULLCA Section 1009.

## ARTICLE 10.
## ACTIONS BY PARTNERS

## SECTION 15910.01. DIRECT ACTIONS BY PARTNER.
(a) Subject to subdivision (b), a partner may maintain a direct action against the limited partnership or another partner for legal or equitable relief, with or without an accounting as to the partnership's activities, to enforce the rights and otherwise protect the interests of the partner, including rights and interests under the partnership agreement or this chapter or arising independently of the partnership relationship.

(b) A partner bringing a direct action under this section is required to plead and prove an actual or threatened injury that is not solely the result of an injury suffered or threatened to be suffered by the limited partnership.

(c) The accrual of, and any time limitation on, a right of action for a remedy under this section is governed by other law. A right to an accounting upon a dissolution and winding up does not revive a claim barred by law.

## Uniform Limited Partnership Act Comment

**Subsection (a)**—Source: RUPA Section 405(b).

**Subsection (b)**—In ordinary contractual situations it is axiomatic that each party to a contract has standing to sue for breach of that contract. Within a limited partnership, however, different circumstances may exist. A partner does not have a direct claim against another partner merely because the other partner has breached the partnership agreement. Likewise a partner's violation of this chapter does not automatically create a direct claim for every other partner. To have standing in his, her, or its own right, a partner plaintiff must be able to show a harm that occurs independently of the harm caused or threatened to be caused to the limited partnership.

The reference to "threatened" harm is intended to encompass claims for injunctive relief and does not relax standards for proving injury.

**SECTION 15910.02. DERIVATIVE ACTION.** A partner may bring a derivative action to enforce a right of a limited partnership if:

(1) the partner first makes a demand on the general partners, requesting that they cause the limited partnership to bring an action to enforce the right, and the general partners do not bring the action within a reasonable time; or

(2) a demand would be futile.

## Uniform Limited Partnership Act Comment

Source—**RULPA Section 1001.**

**SECTION 15910.03. PROPER PLAINTIFF.**

(a) A derivative action may be maintained only by a person that is a partner at the time the action is commenced and:

(1) that was a partner when the conduct giving rise to action occurred; or

(2) whose status as a partner devolved upon the person by operation of law or pursuant to the terms of the partnership agreement from a person that was a partner at the time of that conduct.

(b) Notwithstanding the foregoing, any partner who does not meet the foregoing requirements may nevertheless be allowed in the discretion of the court to maintain the action on a preliminary showing to and determination by the court, by motion and after a hearing, at which the court shall consider such evidence , by affidavit or testimony, as it deems material that (1) there is a strong prima facie case in favor of the claim asserted on behalf of the partnership, (2) no other similar action has been or is likely to be instituted, (3) the plaintiff acquired the shares before there was disclosure to the public and to the plaintiff of the wrongdoing of which plaintiff complains, (4) unless the action can be maintained the defendant may retain a gain derived from the defendant's willful breach of a fiduciary duty, and (5) the requested relief will not result in unjust enrichment of the partnership or any partner.

### Uniform Limited Partnership Act Comment

Source—RULPA Section 1002.

**SECTION 15910.04. PLEADING.** In a derivative action, the complaint must state with particularity:

(1) the date and content of plaintiff's demand and the general partners' response to the demand; or

(2) why demand is excused as futile.

### Uniform Limited Partnership Act Comment

Source—RULPA Section 1003.

**SECTION 15910.05. PROCEEDS AND EXPENSES.**

(a) Except as otherwise provided in subdivision (b):

(1) any proceeds or other benefits of a derivative action, whether by judgment, compromise, or settlement, belong to the limited partnership and not to the derivative plaintiff;

(2) if the derivative plaintiff receives any of those proceeds, the derivative plaintiff shall immediately remit them to the limited partnership.

(b) If a derivative action is successful in whole or in part, the court may award the plaintiff reasonable expenses, including reasonable attorney's fees, from the recovery of the limited partnership.

### Uniform Limited Partnership Act Comment

Source—RULPA Section 1004.

**SECTION 15910.06. FURNISHING OF BOND.**

(a) In any derivative action, at any time within 30 days after service of summons upon the limited partnership or the general partner, the limited partnership or general partner may move the court for an order, upon notice and hearing, requiring the plaintiff to furnish a bond as hereinafter provided. The motion shall be based upon one or both of the following grounds:

(1) That there is no reasonable possibility that the prosecution of the cause of action alleged in the complaint against the moving party will benefit the limited partnership or its partners.

(2) That the moving party, if other than the partnership, did not participate in the transaction complained of in any capacity.

The court on application of the limited partnership or the general partner may, for good cause shown, extend the 30-day period for an additional period or periods not exceeding 60-days.

(b) At the hearing upon any motion pursuant to subdivision (a) the court shall consider such evidence, written or oral, by witnesses or affidavit, as may be material (1) to the ground or grounds upon which the motion is based, or (2) to a determination of the probable reasonable expenses, including attorneys' fees, of the limited partnership and the general partner which will be incurred in defense of the action. If the court determines, after hearing the evidence adduced by the parties, that the moving party has established a probability in support of any of the grounds upon which the motion is based, the court shall fix the amount of the bond, not to exceed fifty thousand dollars ($50,000), to be furnished by the plaintiff for reasonable expenses, including attorneys fees, which may be incurred by the moving party and the limited partnership in connection with the action, including expenses for which the limited partnership may become liable pursuant to subdivision (c) of Section 15904.06. A ruling by the court on the motion shall not be a determination of any issue in the action or of the merits thereof. If the court, upon motion, makes a determination that a bond shall be furnished by the plaintiff as to any one or more defendants, the action shall be dismissed as to the defendant or defendants, unless the bond required by the court has been furnished within such reasonable time as may be fixed by the court.

(c) If the plaintiff shall, either before or after a motion is made pursuant to subdivision (a), or any order or determination pursuant to the motion, furnish a bond in the aggregate amount of fifty thousand dollars ($50,000) to secure the reasonable expenses of the parties entitled to make the motion, the plaintiff has complied with the requirements of this section and with any order for a bond theretofore made, any such motion then pending shall be dismissed and no further additional bond shall be required.

(d) If a motion is filed pursuant to subdivision (a), no pleadings need to be filed by the limited partnership or any other defendant and the prosecution of the action shall be stayed until 10 days after the motion has been disposed of.

**California Code Comment**
*By Phil Jelsma*

**Source:** Cal. Corp. Code Section 17501.

## ARTICLE 11.
## CONVERSION AND MERGER

## SECTION 15911.01. DEFINITIONS.

For purposes of this article, the following definitions apply:

(a) "Converted entity" means the other business entity or foreign other business entity or foreign limited partnership that results from a conversion of a domestic limited partnership under this chapter.

(b) "Converted limited partnership" means a domestic limited partnership that results from a conversion of an other business entity or a foreign other business entity or a foreign limited partnership pursuant to Section 15911.08.

(c) "Converting limited partnership" means a domestic limited partnership that converts to an other business entity or a foreign other business entity or a foreign limited partnership pursuant to this chapter.

(d) "Converting entity" means an other business entity or a foreign other business entity or a foreign limited partnership that converts to a domestic limited partnership pursuant to the terms of Section 15911.08.

(e) "Constituent corporation" means a corporation that is merged with or into one or more limited partnerships or other business entities and that includes a surviving corporation.

(f) "Constituent limited partnership" means a limited partnership that is merged with or into one or more other limited partnerships or other business entities and that includes a surviving limited partnership.

(g) "Constituent other business entity" means an other business entity that is merged with or into one or more limited partnerships and that includes a surviving other business entity.

(h) "Disappearing limited partnership" means a constituent limited partnership that is not the surviving limited partnership.

(i) "Disappearing other business entity" means a constituent other business entity that is not the surviving other business entity.

(j) "Foreign other business entity" means an other business entity formed under the laws of any state other than this state or under the laws of a foreign country.

(k) "Other business entity" means a corporation, general partnership, limited liability company, business trust, real estate investment trust, or unincorporated association (other than a nonprofit association), but excludes a limited partnership.

(l) "Surviving limited partnership" means a limited partnership into which one or more other limited partnerships or other business entities are merged.

(m) "Surviving other business entity" means another business entity into which one or more limited partnerships are merged.

### California Code Comment
#### By Phil Jelsma

Source: **Cal Corp Code Section 15677.1**

## SECTION 15911.02. CONVERSION INTO FOREIGN, OTHER ENTITIES OR FOREIGN LIMITED PARTNERSHIPS: CONDITIONS.

(a) A limited partnership may be converted into another business entity or a foreign other business entity or a foreign limited partnership pursuant to this article if both of the following apply:

(1) Pursuant to a conversion into a domestic or foreign partnership or limited liability company or into a foreign limited partnership, each of the partners of the converting limited partnership receives a percentage interest in the profits and capital of the converted entity equal to that partner's percentage interest in profits and capital of the converting limited partnership as of the effective time of the conversion.

(2) Pursuant to a conversion into an other business entity or foreign other business entity not specified in paragraph (1), both of the following occur: (A) Each limited partnership interest of the same class is treated equally with respect to any distribution of cash, property, rights, interests, or securities of the converted entity, unless all limited partners of the class consent. (B) The nonredeemable limited partnership interests of the converting limited partnership are converted

only into nonredeemable interests or securities of the converted entity, unless all holders of the unredeemable interests consent.

(b) The conversion of a limited partnership to an other business entity or a foreign other business entity or a foreign limited partnership may be effected only if both of the following conditions are satisfied:

(1) The law under which the converted entity will exist expressly permits the formation of that entity pursuant to a conversion.

(2) The limited partnership complies with all other requirements of any other law that applies to conversion to the converted entity.

## California Code Comment
### By Phil Jelsma

Source: **Cal. Corp. Code Section 15677.2**

## SECTION 15911.03. PLAN OF CONVERSION.

(a) A limited partnership that desires to convert to an other business entity or a foreign other business entity or a foreign limited partnership shall approve a plan of conversion. The plan of conversion shall state all of the following:

(1) The terms and conditions of the conversion.

(2) The place of the organization of the converted entity and of the converting limited partnership and the name of the converted entity after conversion.

(3) The manner of converting the limited and general partnership interests of each of the partners into shares of, securities of, or interests in, the converted entity.

(4) The provisions of the governing documents for the converted entity, including the partnership agreement, limited liability company articles of organization and operating agreement, or articles or certificate of incorporation if the converted entity is a corporation, to which the holders of interests in the converted entity are to be bound.

(5) Any other details or provisions that are required by the laws under which the converted entity is organized, or that are desired by the parties.

(b) The plan of conversion shall be approved by all general partners of the converting limited partnership and by a majority in interest of each class of limited partners of the converting limited partnership, unless a greater or lesser approval is required by the partnership agreement of the converting limited partnership.

However, if the limited partners of the limited partnership would become personally liable for any obligations of the converted entity as a result of the conversion, the plan of conversion shall be approved by all of the limited partners of the converting limited partnership, unless the plan of conversion provides that all limited partners will have dissenters' rights as provided in Article 11.5 (commencing with Section 15911.20).

(c) Upon the effectiveness of the conversion, all partners of the converting limited partnership, except those that exercise dissenters' rights as provided in Article 11.5 (commencing with Section 15911.20), shall be deemed parties to any governing documents for the converted entity adopted as part of the plan of conversion, irrespective of whether or not the partner has executed the plan of conversion or the governing documents for the converted entity. Any adoption of governing documents made pursuant thereto shall be effective at the effective time or date of the conversion.

(d) Notwithstanding its prior approval, a plan of conversion may be amended before the conversion takes effect if the amendment is approved by all general partners of the converting limited partnership and, if the amendment changes any of the principal terms of the plan of conversion, the amendment is approved by the limited partners of the converting limited partnership in the same manner and to the same extent as required for the approval of the original plan of conversion.

(e) The general partners of a converting limited partnership may, by unanimous approval at any time before the conversion is effective, in their discretion, abandon a conversion, without further approval by the limited partners, subject to the contractual rights of third parties other than limited partners.

(f) The converted entity shall keep the plan of conversion at the principal place of business of the converted entity if the converted entity is a domestic partnership or foreign other business entity, at the principal executive office of, or registrar or transfer agent of, the converted entity, if the converted entity is a domestic corporation, or at the office at which records are to be kept under Section 17057 if the converted entity is a domestic limited liability company. Upon the request of a partner of a converting limited partnership, the authorized person on behalf of the converted entity shall promptly deliver to the partner or the holder of shares, interests, or other securities, at the expense of the converted entity, a copy of the plan of conversion. A waiver by a partner of the rights provided in this subdivision shall be unenforceable.

**California Code Comment**
*By Phil Jelsma*

Source: **Cal Corp Code Section 15677.3**

## SECTION 15911.04. EFFECTIVE DATE OF CONVERSION; EVIDENCE OF CONVERSION.

(a) A conversion into an other business entity or a foreign other business entity or a foreign limited partnership shall become effective upon the earliest date that all of the following occur:

(1) The plan of conversion is approved by the partners of the converting limited partnership, as provided in Section 15911.03.

(2) All documents required by law to create the converted entity are filed, which documents shall also contain a statement of conversion, if required under Section 15911.06.

(3) The effective date, if set forth in the plan of conversion occurs.

(b) A copy of the statement of partnership authority or articles of organization complying with Section 15911.06, if applicable, duly certified by the Secretary of State, is conclusive evidence of the conversion of the limited partnership.

**California Code Comment**
*By Phil Jelsma*

Source: **Cal Corp Code Section 15677.4**

## SECTION 15911.05. COMPLIANCE WITH OTHER LAWS; SERVICE OF PROCESS.

(a) The conversion of a limited partnership into a foreign limited partnership or foreign other business entity shall be required to comply with Section 15911.02.

(b) If the limited partnership is converting into a foreign limited partnership or foreign other business entity, those conversion proceedings shall be in accordance with the laws of the state or place of organization of the foreign limited partnership or foreign other business entity and the conversion shall become effective in accordance with that law.

(c) (1) To enforce an obligation of a limited partnership that has converted to a foreign limited partnership or foreign other business entity, the Secretary of State shall only be the agent for service of process in an action or proceeding against that converted foreign entity, if the agent designated for the service of process for that entity is a natural person and cannot be found with due diligence or if the agent is a corporation and no person, to whom delivery may be made, may be located with due diligence, or if no agent has been designated and if no one of the officers, partners, managers, members, or agents of that entity may be located after diligent search, and it is so shown by affidavit to the satisfaction of the court. The court then may make an order that service be made by personal delivery to the Secretary of State or to an assistant or deputy Secretary of State of two copies of the process together with two copies of the order, and the order shall set forth an address to which the process shall be sent by the Secretary of State. Service in this manner is deemed complete on the 10th day after delivery of the process to the Secretary of State.

(2) Upon receipt of the process and order and the fee set forth in Section 12206 of the Government Code, the Secretary of State shall provide notice to that entity of the service of the process by forwarding by certified mail, return receipt requested, a copy of the process and order to the address specified in the order.

(3) The Secretary of State shall keep a record of all process served upon the Secretary of State and shall record therein the time of service and the Secretary of State's action with respect thereto. The certificate of the Secretary of State, under the Secretary of State's official seal, certifying to the receipt of process, the providing of notice thereof to that entity, and the forwarding of the process shall be competent and prima facie evidence of the matters stated therein.

### California Code Comment
*By Phil Jelsma*

Source: **Cal Corp Code Section 15677.5**

## SECTION 15911.06. CERTIFICATE OR STATEMENT OF CONVERSION.

(a) Upon conversion of a limited partnership, one of the following applies:

(1) If the limited partnership is converting into a domestic limited liability company, a statement of conversion shall be completed on the articles of organization for the converted entity and shall be filed with the Secretary of State.

(2) If the limited partnership is converting into a domestic partnership, a statement of conversion shall be completed on the statement of partnership authority for the converted entity. If no statement of partnership authority is filed, a certificate of conversion shall be filed separately with the Secretary of State.

(3) If the limited partnership is converting into a domestic corporation, a statement of conversion shall be completed on the articles of incorporation for the converted entity and shall be filed with the Secretary of State.

(4) If the limited partnership is converting to a foreign limited partnership or foreign other business entity, a certificate of conversion shall be filed with the Secretary of State.

(b) Any certificate or statement of conversion shall be executed and acknowledged by all general partners, unless a lesser number is provided in the certificate of limited partnership, and shall set forth all of the following:

(1) The name and the Secretary of State's file number of the converting limited partnership.

(2) A statement that the principal terms of the plan of conversion were approved by a vote of the partners, that equaled or exceeded the vote required under Section 15911.03, specifying each class entitled to vote and the percentage vote required of each class.

(3) The form of organization of the converted entity.

(4) The mailing address of the converted entity's agent for service of process and the chief executive office of the converted entity.

(c) The filing with the Secretary of State of a certificate of conversion or a statement of partnership authority, articles of organization, or articles of incorporation containing a statement of conversion as set forth in subdivision (a) shall have the effect of the filing of a certificate of cancellation by the converting limited partnership, and no converting limited partnership that has made the filing is required to file a certificate of cancellation under Section 15902.03 as a result of that conversion.

### California Code Comment
*By Phil Jelsma*

Source: **Cal Corp Code Section 15677.6**

## SECTION 15911.07. REAL PROPERTY; ESTABLISHMENT OF RECORD OWNERSHIPS.

(a) Whenever a limited partnership or other business entity having any real property in this state converts into a limited partnership or an other business entity pursuant to the laws of this state or of the state or place in which the limited partnership or other business entity was organized, and the laws of the state or place of organization, including this state, of the converting limited partnership or other converting entity provide substantially that the conversion vests in the converted limited partnership or other converted entity all the real property of the converting limited partnership or other converting entity, the filing for record in the office of the county recorder of any county in this state in which any of the real property of the converting limited partnership or other converting entity is located of either of the following shall evidence record ownership in the converted limited partnership or other converted entity of all interest of the converting limited partnership or other converting entity in and to the real property located in that county?: (1) A certificate of conversion or statement of partnership authority, a certificate of limited partnership, articles of incorporation, or articles of organization complying with Section 15911.06, in the form prescribed and certified by the Secretary of State. (2) A copy of a certificate of conversion or a statement of partnership authority, certificate of limited partnership, articles of organization, articles of incorporation, or other certificate or document evidencing the creation of a foreign other business entity or foreign limited partnership by conversion, containing a statement of conversion, certified by the Secretary of State or an authorized public official of the state or place pursuant to the laws of which the conversion is effected.

(b) A filed and, if appropriate, recorded certificate of conversion or a statement of partnership authority, certificate of limited partnership, articles of organization, articles or certificate of incorporation, or other certificate evidencing the creation of a foreign other business entity or foreign limited partnership by conversion, containing a statement of conversion, filed pursuant to subdivision (a) of Section 15911.06, stating the name of the converting limited partnership or other converting entity in whose name property was held before the conversion and the name of the converted entity or converted limited partnership, but not containing all of the other information required by Section 15911.06, operates with respect to the entities named to the extent provided in subdivision (a).

(c) Recording of a certificate of conversion, or a statement of partnership authority, certificate of limited partnership, articles of organization, articles of incorporation, or other certificate evidencing the creation of another business entity or a limited partnership by conversion, containing a statement of conversion, in accordance with subdivision (a), shall create, in favor of bona fide purchasers or encumbrances for value, a conclusive presumption that the conversion was validly completed.

### California Code Comment
*By Phil Jelsma*

Source: **Cal Corp Code Section 15677.7** A conversion is not a transfer of property.

## SECTION 15911.08. CONVERSION TO A DOMESTIC LIMITED PARTNERSHIP.

(a) An other business entity or a foreign other business entity or a foreign limited partnership may be converted to a domestic limited partnership pursuant to this article only if the converting entity is authorized by the laws under which it is organized to effect the conversion.

(b) An other business entity or a foreign other business entity or a foreign limited partnership that desires to convert into a domestic limited partnership shall approve a plan of conversion or another instrument as is required to be approved to effect the conversion pursuant to the laws under which that entity is organized.

(c) The conversion of an other business entity or a foreign other business entity or a foreign limited partnership into a domestic limited partnership shall be approved by the number or percentage of the partners, members, shareholders, or holders of interest of the converting entity as is required by the laws under which that entity is organized, or a greater or lesser percentage, subject to applicable laws, as set forth in the converting entity's partnership agreement, articles of organization, operating agreement, articles or certificate of incorpo ration, or other governing document.

(d) The conversion by an other business entity or a foreign other business entity or a foreign limited partnership into a domestic limited partnership shall be effective under this article at the time the conversion is effective under the laws under which the converting entity is organized, as long as a certificate of limited partnership containing a statement of conversion has been filed with the Secretary of State. If the converting entity's governing law is silent as to the effectiveness of the conversion, the conversion shall be effective upon the completion of all acts required under this title to form a limited partnership.

(e) The filing with the Secretary of State of a certificate of conversion or a certificate of limited partnership containing a statement of conversion pursuant to subdivision (a) shall have the effect of the filing of a certificate of cancellation by the converting foreign limited partnership or foreign limited liability company and no converting foreign limited partnership or foreign limited liability company that has made the filing is required to file a certificate of cancellation under Section 15902.03 or 17455 as a result of that conversion. If a converting other business entity is a foreign corporation qualified to transact business in this state, the foreign corporation shall, by virtue of the filing, automatically surrender its right to transact intrastate business.

## California Code Comment
### By Phil Jelsma

Source: **Cal Corp Code Section 15677.8**. A conversion is not a transfer of property.

## SECTION 15911.09. CONVERSION TO ANOTHER ENTITY.

(a) An entity that converts into another entity pursuant to this article is for all purposes other than for the purposes of Part 10 (commencing with Section 17001) of Part 10.20 (commencing with Section 18401)of, and Part 11 (commencing with Section 23001) of, Division 2 of the Revenue and Taxation Code, the same entity that existed before the conversion and the conversion shall not be deemed a transfer of property.

(b) Upon a conversion taking effect, all of the following apply:

(1) All the rights and property, whether real, personal, or mixed, of the converting entity or converting limited partnership are vested in the converted entity or converted limited partnership.

(2) All debts, liabilities, and obligations of the converting entity or converting limited partnership continue as debts, liabilities, and obligations of the converted entity or converted limited partnership.

(3) All rights of creditors and liens upon the property of the converting entity or converting limited partnership shall be preserved unimpaired and remain enforceable against the converted entity or converted limited partnership to the same extent as against the converting entity or converting limited partnership as if the conversion had not occurred.

(4) Any action or proceeding pending by or against the converting entity or converting limited partnership may be continued against the converted entity or converted limited partnership as if the conversion had not occurred.

(c) A partner of a converting limited partnership is liable for the following:

(1) All obligations of the converting limited partnership for which the partner was personally liable before the conversion.

(2) All obligations of the converted entity incurred after the conversion takes effect, but those obligations may be satisfied only out of property of the entity if that partner is a limited partner, or a shareholder in a corporation, or unless expressly provided otherwise in the articles of organization or other governing documents, a member of a limited liability company, or a holder of equity securities in another converted entity if the holders of equity securities in that entity are not personally liable for the obligations of that entity under the law under which the entity is organized or its governing documents.

(d) A partner of a converted limited partnership remains liable for any and all obligations of the converting entity for which the partner was personally liable before the conversion, but only to the extent that the partner was liable for the obligations of the converting entity prior to the conversion.

(e) If the other party to a transaction with the limited partnership reasonably believes when entering the transaction that the limited partner is a general partner, the limited partner is liable for an obligation incurred by the limited partnership within 90 days after the conversion takes effect. The limited partner's liability for all other obligations of the limited partnership incurred after the conversion takes effect is that of a limited partner.

### California Code Comment
*By Phil Jelsma*

Source: **Cal Corp Code Section 14577.9**. A conversion is not a transfer of property.

**SECTION 15911.10. MERGERS.** Mergers of limited partnerships shall be governed by Sections 15911.11 to 15911.19 inclusive.

**SECTION 15911.11. MERGERS; CONDITIONS.** The following entities may be merged pursuant to this article:

(a) Two or more limited partnerships into one limited partnership.

(b) One or more limited partnerships and one or more other business entities into one of those other business entities.

(c) One or more limited partnerships and one or more other business entities into one limited partnership.

Notwithstanding this section, the merger of any number of limited partnerships with any number of other business entities may be effected only if the other business entities that are organized in California are authorized by the laws under which they are organized to effect the merger, and

(1) if a limited partnership is the surviving limited partnership, the foreign other business entities are not prohibited by the laws under which they are organized from effecting that merger, and

(2) if a foreign limited partnership or foreign other business entity is the survivor of the merger, the laws of the jurisdiction under which the survivor is organized authorize that merger. Notwithstanding the first sentence of this paragraph, if one or more domestic corporations is also a party to the merger described in that sentence, the merger may be effected only if, with respect to any foreign other business entity that is a corporation, the foreign corporation is authorized by the laws under which it is organized to effect that merger.

### California Code Comment
*By Phil Jelsma*

Source: **Cal Corp Code Section 15678.1**

## SECTION 15911.12. AGREEMENT; APPROVAL; PARTIES; CONTRACTS; LIMITED PARTNERSHIP INTERESTS; DISTRIBUTIONS; CONVERSIONS; AMENDMENTS; ABANDONMENT; DELIVERY.

(a) Each limited partnership and other business entity that desires to merge shall approve an agreement of merger. The agreement of merger shall be approved by all general partners of each constituent limited partnership and the principal terms of the merger shall be approved by a majority in interest of each class of limited partners of each constituent limited partnership, unless a greater approval is required by the partnership agreement of the constituent limited partnership. Notwithstanding the previous sentence, if the limited partners of any constituent limited partnership become personally liable for any obligations of a constituent limited partnership or constituent other business entity as a result of the merger, the principal terms of the agreement of merger shall be approved by all of the limited partners of the constituent limited partnership, unless the agreement of merger provides that all limited partners will have the dissenters' rights provided in Article 11.5 (commencing with Section 15911.20). The agreement of merger shall be approved on behalf of each constituent other business entity by those persons required to approve the merger by the laws under which it is organized. Other persons, including a parent of a constituent limited partnership, may be parties to the agreement of merger. The agreement of merger shall state:

(1) The terms and conditions of the merger.

(2) The name and place of organization of the surviving limited partnership or surviving other business entity, and of each disappearing limited partnership and disappearing other business entity, and the agreement of merger may change the name of the surviving limited partnership, which new name may be the same as or similar to the name of a disappearing domestic or foreign limited partnership, subject to Section 15901.08.

(3) The manner of converting the partnership interests of each of the constituent limited partnerships into interests, shares, or other securities of the surviving limited partnership or surviving other business entity, and if partnership interests of any of the constituent limited partnerships are not to be converted solely into interests, shares, or other securities of the surviving limited partnership or surviving other business entity, the cash, property, rights, interests, or securities that the holders of the partnership interests are to receive in exchange for the partnership interests, which cash, property, rights, interests, or securities may be in addition to or in lieu of interests, shares, or other securities of the surviving limited partnership or surviving other business entity, or that the partnership interests are canceled without consideration.

(4) Any other details or provisions that are required by the laws under which any constituent other business entity is organized, including, if a domestic corporation is a party to the merger, subdivision (b) of Section 1113.

(5) Any other details or provisions that are desired, including, without limitation, a provision for the treatment of fractional partnership interests.

(b) Each limited partnership interest of the same class of any constituent limited partnership, other than a limited partnership interest in another constituent limited partnership that is being canceled and that is held by a constituent limited partnership or its parent or a limited partnership of which the constituent limited partnership is a parent shall, unless all limited partners of the class consent, be treated equally with respect to any distribution of cash, property, rights, interests, or securities. Notwithstanding this subdivision, except in a merger of a limited partnership with a limited partnership in which it controls at least 90 percent of the limited partnership interests entitled to vote with respect to the merger, the unredeemable limited partnership interests of a constituent limited partnership may be converted only into unredeemable interests or securities of the surviving limited partnership or other business entity or a parent if a constituent limited partnership or a constituent other business entity or its parent owns, directly or indirectly, prior to the merger, limited partnership interests of another constituent limited partnership or interests or securities of a constituent other business entity representing more than 50 percent of the interests or securities entitled to vote with respect to the merger of the other constituent limited partnership or constituent other business entity or more than 50 percent of the voting power, as defined in Section 194.5, of a constituent other business entity that is a domestic corporation, unless all of the limited partners of the class consent. This subdivision shall apply only to constituent limited partnerships with over 35 limited partners.

(c) Notwithstanding its prior approval, an agreement of merger may be amended prior to the filing of the certificate of merger or the agreement of merger, as provided in Section 15911.14, if the amendment is approved by the general partners of each constituent limited partnership in the same manner as required for approval of the original agreement of merger and, if the amendment changes any of the principal terms of the agreement of merger, the amendment is approved by the limited partners of each constituent limited partnership in the same manner and to the same extent as required for the approval of the original agreement of merger, and by each of the constituent other business entities.

(d) The general partners of a constituent limited partnership may, in their discretion, abandon a merger, subject to the contractual rights, if any, of third parties, including other constituent limited partnerships and constituent other business entities, without further approval by the limited partnership interests, at any time before the merger is effective.

(e) An agreement of merger approved in accordance with subdivision (a) may

(1) effect any amendment to the partnership agreement of any constituent limited partnership or

(2) effect the adoption of a new partnership agreement for a constituent limited partnership if it is the surviving limited partnership in the merger. Any amendment to a partnership agreement or adoption of a new partnership agreement made pursuant to the foregoing sentence shall be effective at the effective time or date of the merger. Notwithstanding the above provisions of this subdivision, if a greater number of limited partners is required to approve an amendment to the partnership agreement of a constituent limited partnership than is required to approve the agreement of merger pursuant to subdivision (a), and the number of limited partners that approve the agreement of merger is less than the number of limited partners required to approve an amendment to the partnership agreement of the constituent limited partnership, any amendment to the partnership agreement or adoption of a new partnership agreement of that constituent limited partnership made pursuant to the first sentence of this subdivision shall be effective only if the agreement of merger provides that all of the limited partners shall have the dissenters' rights provided in Article 7.6 (commencing with Section 15911.20).

(f) The surviving limited partnership or surviving other business entity shall keep the agreement of merger at its designated office or at the business address specified in paragraph (5) of subdivision (a) of Section 15911.14, as applicable, and, upon the request of a limited partner of a constituent limited partnership or a holder of shares, interests, or other securities of a constituent other business entity, the general partners of the surviving limited partnership or the authorized person of the surviving other business entity shall promptly deliver to the limited partner or the holder of shares, interests, or other securities, at the expense of the surviving limited partnership or surviving other business entity, a copy of the agreement of merger. A waiver by a partner or holder of shares, interests, or other securities of the rights provided in this subdivision shall be unenforceable.

## California Code Comment
### By Phil Jelsma

Source: **Cal Corp Code Section 15678.2**

**SECTION 15911.13. APPROVAL OF TERMS AND CONDITIONS OF TRANSACTION BY COMMISSIONER INAPPLICATION OF SUBDIVISION (b) OF SECTION 15678.2.** Subdivision (b) of Section 15911.12 shall not apply to any transaction if the commissioner has approved the terms and conditions of the transaction and the fairness of such terms and conditions pursuant to Section 25142.

## California Code Comment
### By Phil Jelsma

Source: **Cal Corp Code Section 15678.3**

**SECTION 15911.14. CERTIFICATE OF MERGER; FILING; EXECUTION; CONTENTS; EFFECT; AGREEMENT OF MERGER FILING.**

(a) If the surviving entity is a limited partnership or an other business entity, other than a corporation in a merger in which a domestic corporation is a constituent party, after approval of a merger by the constituent limited partnerships and any constituent other business entities, the constituent limited partnerships and constituent other business entities shall file a certificate of merger in the office of, and on a form prescribed by, the Secretary of State. The certificate of merger shall be executed and acknowledged by each domestic constituent limited partnership by all general partners unless a lesser number is provided in the certificate of limited partnership of the domestic constituent limited partnership and by each foreign constituent limited partnership by one or more general partners, and by each constituent other business entity by those persons required to execute the certificate of merger by the laws under which the constituent other business entity is organized. The certificate of merger shall set forth all of the following:

(1) The names and the Secretary of State's file numbers, if any, of each of the constituent limited partnerships and constituent other business entities, separately identifying the disappearing limited partnerships and disappearing other business entities and the surviving limited partnership or surviving other business entity.

(2) If a vote of the limited partners was required under Section

15911.12, a statement setting forth the total number of outstanding interests of each class entitled to vote on the merger and that the principal terms of the agreement of merger were approved by a vote of the number of interests of each class which equaled or exceeded the vote required, specifying each class entitled to vote and the percentage vote required of each class.

(3) If the surviving entity is a limited partnership and not an other business entity, any change required to the information set forth in the certificate of limited partnership of the surviving limited partnership resulting from the merger, including any change in the name of the surviving limited partnership resulting from the merger. The filing of a certificate of merger setting forth any such changes to the certificate of limited partnership of the surviving limited partnership shall have the effect of the filing of a certificate of amendment by the surviving limited partnership, and the surviving limited partnership need not file a certificate of amendment under Section 15902.02 to reflect those changes.

(4) The future effective date or time, which shall be a date or time certain not more than 90 days subsequent to the date of filing of the merger, if the merger is not to be effective upon the filing of the certificate of merger with the office of the Secretary of State.

(5) If the surviving entity is an other business entity or a foreign limited partnership, the full name of the entity, type of entity, legal jurisdiction in which the entity was organized and by whose laws its internal affairs are governed, and the address of the principal place of business of the entity.

(6) Any other information required to be stated in the certificate of merger by the laws under which each constituent other business entity is organized, including, if a domestic corporation is a party to the merger, paragraph (2) of subdivision (g) of Section 1113. If the surviving entity is a foreign limited partnership in a merger in which a domestic corporation is a disappearing other business entity, a copy of the agreement of merger and attachments as required under paragraph (1) of subdivision (g) of Section 1113 shall be filed at the same time as the filing of the certificate of merger.

(b) If the surviving entity is a domestic corporation or a foreign corporation in a merger in which a domestic corporation is a constituent party, after approval of the merger by the constituent limited partnerships and constituent other business entities, the surviving corporation shall file in the office of the Secretary of State a copy of the agreement of merger and attachments required under paragraph (1) of subdivision (g) of Section 1113. The certificate of merger shall be executed and acknowledged by each domestic constituent limited partnership by all general partners, unless a lesser number is provided in the certificate of limited partnership of the domestic constituent limited partnership.

(c) A certificate of merger or the agreement of merger, as is applicable under subdivision (a) or (b), shall have the effect of the filing of a certificate of cancellation for each disappearing limited partnership, and no disappearing limited partnership need file a certificate of cancellation under Section 15902.03 as a result of the merger.

(d) If the organization disappearing into the other business entity is a foreign corporation qualified to transact intrastate business in this state, a certificate of satisfaction of the Franchise Tax Board as required by Section 23334 of the Revenue and Taxation Code shall be filed with the certificate of merger or agreement of merger, as is applicable under subdivision (a) or (b). By the filing of the certificate of merger or agreement of merger, as is applicable, the foreign corporation shall automatically surrender its right to transact intrastate business.

## California Code Comment
*By Phil Jelsma*

Source: **Cal Corp Code Section 15678.4**

## SECTION 15911.15. EFFECTIVE DATE OF MERGER; CONCLUSIVE EVIDENCE OF MERGER; CERTIFIED COPY OF MERGER AGREEMENT.

(a) Unless a future effective date or time is provided in a certificate of merger or the agreement of merger, if an agreement of merger is required to be filed under Section 15911.14, in which event the merger shall be effective at that future effective date or time, a merger shall be effective upon the filing of the certificate of merger or the agreement of merger, as is applicable, in the office of the Secretary of State.

(b)(1) For all purposes, a copy of the certificate of merger duly certified by the Secretary of State is conclusive evidence of the merger of (A) the constituent limited partnerships, either by themselves or together with constituent other business entities, into the surviving other business entity, or (B) the constituent limited partnerships or the constituent other business entities, or both, into the surviving limited partnership.

(2) In a merger in which the surviving entity is a corporation in a merger in which a domestic corporation and a domestic limited partnership are parties to the merger, a copy of an agreement of merger certified on or after the effective date by an official having custody thereof has the same force in evidence as the original and, except as against the state, is conclusive evidence of the performance of all conditions precedent to the merger, the existence on the effective date of the surviving corporation, and the performance of the conditions necessary to the adoption of any amendment to the articles of incorporation of the surviving corporation, if applicable, contained in the agreement of merger.

### California Code Comment
*By Phil Jelsma*

Source: **Cal Corp Code Section 15678.5**

## SECTION 15911.16. SURVIVING LIMITED PARTNERSHIP SUCCESSION TO RIGHTS AND PROPERTY AND DEBT AND LIABILITIES OF DISAPPEARING ENTITY LIENS ON PROPERTY; PENDING ACTION.

(a) Upon a merger of limited partnerships or limited partnerships and other business entities pursuant to this chapter, the separate existence of the disappearing limited partnerships and disappearing other business entities ceases and the surviving limited partnership or surviving other business entity shall succeed, without other transfer, act or deed, to all the rights and property, whether real, personal, or mixed, of each of the disappearing limited partnerships and disappearing other business entities, and shall be subject to all the debts and liabilities of each in the same manner as if the surviving limited partnership or surviving other business entity had itself incurred them.

(b) All rights of creditors and all liens upon the property of each of the constituent limited partnerships and constituent other business entities shall be preserved unimpaired and may be enforced against the surviving limited partnership or the surviving other business entity to the same extent as if the debt, liability, or duty which gave rise to that lien had been incurred or contracted by the surviving limited partnership or the surviving other business entity, provided that such liens upon the property of a disappearing limited partnership or disappearing other business entity shall be limited to the property affected thereby immediately prior to the time the merger is effective.

(c) Any action or proceeding pending by or against any disappearing limited partnership or disappearing other business entity may be prosecuted to judgment, which shall bind the surviving limited partnership or surviving other business entity, or the surviving limited partnership or surviving other business entity may be proceeded against or be substituted in the place of the disappearing limited partnership or disappearing other business entity.

(d) Nothing in this article is intended to affect the liability a general partner of a disappearing limited partnership may have in connection with the debts and liabilities of the disappearing limited partnership existing prior to the time the merger is effective.

### California Code Comment
#### By Phil Jelsma

Source: **Cal Corp Code Section 15678.6**

## SECTION 15911.17. FOREIGN LIMITED PARTNERSHIP; MERGER WITH DOMESTIC ENTITIES; CONDITIONS; SURVIVING ENTITIES; LAW GOVERNING; EFFECTIVE DATE.

(a) The merger of any number of domestic limited partnerships with any number of foreign limited partnerships or foreign other business entities shall be required to comply with Section 15911.10.

(b) If the surviving entity is a domestic limited partnership or a domestic other business entity, the merger proceedings with respect to that limited partnership or other business entity and any domestic disappearing limited partnership shall conform to the provisions of this chapter governing the merger of domestic limited partnerships, but if the surviving entity is a foreign limited partnership or a foreign other business entity, then, subject to the requirements of subdivision (d) and Article 11.5 (commencing with Section 15911.20) and, with respect to any domestic constituent corporation, Section 1113 and Chapters 12 (commencing with Section 1200) and 13 (commencing with Section 1300) of Division 1 of Title 1, the merger proceedings may be in accordance with the laws of the state or place of organization of the surviving limited partnership or surviving other business entity.

(c) If the surviving entity is a domestic limited partnership or domestic other business entity, other than a domestic corporation, the certificate of merger shall be filed as provided in subdivision

(a) of Section 15911.14, and thereupon, subject to subdivision (a) of Section 15911.15, the merger shall be effective as to each domestic constituent limited partnership and domestic constituent other business entity. If the surviving entity is a domestic corporation, the agreement of merger with attachments shall be filed as provided in subdivision (b) of Section 15911.14, and thereupon, subject to subdivision (a) of Section 15911.15, the merger shall be effective as to each domestic constituent limited partnership and domestic constituent other business entity unless another effective date is provided in Chapter 11 (commencing with Section 1100) of Division 1 of Title 1, with respect to any constituent corporation or constituent limited partnership.

(d) If the surviving entity is a foreign limited partnership or foreign other business entity, the merger shall become effective in accordance with the law of the jurisdiction in which the surviving limited partnership or surviving other business entity is organized, but shall be effective as to any domestic disappearing limited partnership as of the time of effectiveness in the foreign jurisdiction upon the filing in this state of a certificate of merger or agreement of merger as provided in Section 15911.14.

(e) If a merger described in subdivision (c) or (d) also includes a foreign disappearing limited partnership previously registered for the transaction of intrastate business in this state pursuant to Section 15909.02, the filing of the certificate of merger or agreement of merger, as is applicable under Section 15911.14, automatically has the effect of a cancellation of registration for that foreign limited partnership pursuant to Section 15909.06 without the necessity of the filing of a certificate of cancellation.

(f) The provisions of subdivision (b) of Section 15911.12 and Article 11.5 (commencing with Section 15911.20) apply to the rights of the limited partners of any of the constituent limited partnerships that are domestic limited partnerships and of any domestic limited partnership that is a parent of any foreign constituent limited partnership.

## California Code Comment
### By Phil Jelsma

Source: **Cal Corp Code Section 15678.7**

## SECTION 15911.18. REAL PROPERTY RIGHTS; RECORD OF OWNERSHIP; FILING REQUIREMENTS. Whenever a do-

mestic or foreign limited partnership or other business entity having any real property in this state merges with another limited partnership or other business entity pursuant to the laws of this state or of the state or place in which any constituent limited partnership or constituent other business entity was organized, and the laws of the state or place of organization, including this state of any disappearing limited partnership or disappearing other business entity provide substantially that the making and filing of the agreement of merger or certificate of merger vests in the surviving limited partnership or surviving other business entity all the real property of any disappearing limited partnership and disappearing other business entity, the filing for record in the office of the county recorder of any county in this state in which any of the real property of the disappearing limited partnership or disappearing other business entity is located of either of the following shall evidence record ownership in the surviving limited partnership or surviving other business entity of all interest of such disappearing limited partnership or disappearing other business entity in and to the real property located in that county: (a) A certificate of merger certified by the Secretary of State, or other certificate prescribed by the Secretary of State, (b) A copy of the agreement of merger or certificate of merger, certified by the Secretary of State or an authorized public official of the state or place pursuant to the laws of which the merger is effected.

### California Code Comment
*By Phil Jelsma*

Source: **Cal Corp Code Section 15678.8**

**SECTION 15911.19. RECORDING OF CERTIFICATE; CONCLUSIVE PRESUMPTIVE OF MERGER.** Recording of the certificate of merger in accordance with Section 15911.18 shall create, in favor of bona fide purchasers or encumbrancers for value, a conclusive presumption that the merger was validly completed.

### California Code Comment
*By Phil Jelsma*

Source: **Cal Corp Code Section 15678.9**

## ARTICLE 11.5
## DISSENTING LIMITED PARTNERS' RIGHTS

### SECTION 15911.20. DEFINITIONS.

(a) For purposes of this article, "reorganization" refers to any of the following:

(1) A conversion pursuant to Article 11 (commencing with Section 15911.01).

(2) A merger pursuant to Article 11 (commencing with Section 15911.10).

(3) The acquisition by one limited partnership in exchange, in whole or in part, for its partnership interests (or the partnership interests or equity securities of a partnership or other business entity that is in control of the acquiring limited partnership) of partnership interests or equity securities of another limited partnership or other business entity if, immediately after the acquisition, the acquiring limited partnership has control of the other limited partnership or other business entity.

(4) The acquisition by one limited partnership in exchange in whole or in part for its partnership interests (or the partnership interests or equity securities of a partnership or other business entity which is in control of the acquiring limited partnership) or for its debts securities (or debt securities of a limited partnership or other business entity which is in control of the acquiring limited partnership) which are not adequately secured and which have a maturity date in excess of five years after the consummation of the acquisition, or both, of all or substantially all of the assets of another limited partnership or other business entity.

(b) For purposes of this article, "control" means the possession, direct or indirect, of the power to direct or cause the direction of the management and policies of a limited partnership or other business entity.

### California Code Comment
*By Phil Jelsma*

Source: **Cal. Corp. Code Section 15679.1.**

### SECTION 15911.21. LIMITED PARTNERS' RIGHT TO REQUIRE PARTNERSHIPS TO PURCHASE DISSENTING INTEREST.

(a) If the approval of outstanding limited partnership interests is required for a limited partnership to participate in a reorganization, pursuant to the limited partnership agreement of the partnership, or otherwise, then each limited partner of the limited partnership holding those interests may, by complying with this article, require the limited partnership to purchase for cash, at its fair market value, the interest owned by the limited partner in the limited partnership, if the interest is a dissenting interest as defined in subdivision (b). The fair market value shall be determined as of the day before the first announcement of the terms of the proposed reorganization, excluding any appreciation or depreciation in consequence of the proposed reorganization.

(b) As used in this article, "dissenting interest" means the interest of a limited partner that satisfies all of the following conditions:

(1) Either:

(A) Was not, immediately prior to the reorganization, either (i) listed on any national securities exchange certified by the Commissioner of Corporations under subdivision (o) of Section 25100, or (ii) listed on the list of OTC margin stocks issued by the Board of Governors of the Federal Reserve System, provided that in either such instance the limited partnership whose outstanding interests are so listed provides, in its notice to limited partners requesting their approval of the proposed reorganization, a summary of the provisions of this section and Sections 15911.22, 15911.23, 15911.24 and 15911.25; or

(B) If the interest is of a class of interests listed as described in clause (i) or (ii) of subparagraph (A), demands for payment are filed with respect to 5 percent or more of the outstanding interests of that class.

(2) Was outstanding on the date for the determination of limited partners entitled to vote on the reorganization.

(3) (A) Was not voted in favor of the reorganization, or (B) if the interest is described in clause (i) or (ii) of subparagraph (A) of paragraph (1), was voted against the reorganization; provided, however, that clause (A) rather than clause (B) of this paragraph applies in any event where the approval for the proposed reorganization is sought by written consent rather than at a meeting.

(4) The limited partner has demanded that it be purchased by the limited partnership at its fair market value in accordance with Section 15911.22.

(5) The limited partner has submitted it for endorsement, if applicable, in accordance with Section 15911.23.

(c) As used in this article, "dissenting limited partner" means the recordholder of a dissenting interest, and includes an assignee of record of such an interest.

### California Code Comment
*By Phil Jelsma*

Source: **Cal. Corp. Code Section 15679.2.**

## SECTION 15911.22. PURCHASE OF DISSENTING INTERESTS - NOTICE OF REORGANIZATION.

(a) If limited partners have a right under Section 15911.21, subject to compliance with paragraphs (4) and (5) of subdivision (b) thereof, to require the limited partnership to purchase their limited partnership interests for cash, such limited partnership shall mail to each such limited partner a notice of the approval of the reorganization by the requisite vote or consent of the limited partners, within 10 days after the date of such approval, accompanied by a copy of this section and Sections 15911.21, 15911.23, 15911.24 and 15911.25, a statement of the price determined by the limited partnership to represent the fair market value of its outstanding interests, and a brief description of the procedure to be followed if the limited partner desires to exercise the limited partner's rights under such sections. The statement of price constitutes an offer by the limited partnership to purchase at the price stated any dissenting interests as defined in subdivision (b) of Section 15911.21, unless they lose their status as dissenting interests under Section 15911.30.

(b) Any limited partner who has a right to require the limited partnership to purchase the limited partner's interest for cash under Section 15911.21, subject to compliance with paragraphs (4) and (5) of subdivision (b) thereof, and who desires the limited partnership to purchase such interest, shall make written demand upon the limited partnership for the purchase of such interest and the payment to the limited partner in cash of its fair market value. The demand is not effective for any purpose unless it is received by the limited partnership or any transfer agent thereof (1) in the case of interests described in clause (i) or (ii) of subparagraph (A) of paragraph (1) of subdivision (b) of Section 15911.21, not later than the date of the limited partners' meeting to vote upon the reorganization, or

(2) in any other case, within 30 days after the date on which notice of the approval of the reorganization by the requisite vote or consent of the limited partners is mailed by the limited partnership to the limited partners.

(c) The demand shall state the number or amount of the limited partner's interest in the limited partnership and shall contain a statement of what such limited partner claims to be the fair market value of that interest on the day before the announcement of the proposed reorganization. The statement of fair market value constitutes an offer by the limited partner to sell the interest at such price.

### California Code Comment
*By Phil Jelsma*

Source: **Cal Corp Code Section 15679.3.**

### SECTION 15911.23. PURCHASE OF DISSENTING INTERESTS - SUBMISSION OF CERTIFICATE OR WRITTEN NOTICE OF LIMITED PARTNERSHIP INTEREST.
Within 30 days after the date on which notice of the approval of the outstanding interests of the limited partnership is mailed to the limited partner pursuant to subdivision (a) of Section 15911.22, the limited partner shall submit to the limited partnership at its principal office or at the office of any transfer agent thereof, (a) if the interest is evidenced by a certificate, the limited partner's certificate representing the interest which the limited partner demands that the limited partnership purchase, to be stamped or endorsed with a statement that the interest is a dissenting interest or to be exchanged for certificates of appropriate denominations so stamped or endorsed, or (b) if the interest is not evidenced by a certificate, written notice of the number or amount of interest which the limited partner demands that the limited partnership purchase. Upon subsequent transfers of the dissenting interest on the books of the limited partnership, the new certificates or other written statement issued therefor shall bear a like statement, together with the name of the original holder of the dissenting interest.

### California Code Comment
*By Phil Jelsma*

Source: **Cal Corp Code Section 15679.4**

### SECTION 15911.24. AGREEMENT ON PURCHASE OF DISSENTING LIMITED PARTNERSHIP INTEREST.
(a) If the limited partnership and the dissenting limited partner

agree that such limited partner's interest is a dissenting interest and agree upon the price to be paid for the dissenting interest, the dissenting limited partner is entitled to the agreed price with interest thereon at the legal rate on judgments from the date of consummation of the reorganization. All agreements fixing the fair market value of any dissenting limited partner's interest as between the limited partnership and such limited partner shall be in writing and filed in the records of the limited partnership.

(b) Subject to the provisions of Section 15911.27, payment of the fair market value for a dissenting interest shall be made within 30 days after the amount thereof has been agreed to or within 30 days after any statutory or contractual conditions to the reorganization are satisfied, whichever is later, and in the case of dissenting interests evidenced by certificates of interest, subject to surrender of such certificates of interest, unless provided otherwise by agreement.

### California Code Comment
*By Phil Jelsma*

Source: **Cal Corp Code Section 15679.5.**

## SECTION 15911.25. DISAGREEMENT ON PURCHASE OF DISSENTING LIMITED PARTNERSHIP INTEREST JUDICIAL RELIEF.

(a) If the limited partnership denies that a limited partnership interest is a dissenting interest, or the limited partnership and a dissenting limited partner fail to agree upon the fair market value of a dissenting interest, then such limited partner or any interested limited partnership, within six months after the date on which notice of the approval of the reorganization by the requisite vote or consent of the limited partners was mailed to the limited partner, but not thereafter, may file a complaint in the superior court of the proper county praying the court to determine whether the interest is a dissenting interest, or the fair market value of the dissenting interest, or both, or may intervene in any action pending on such a complaint.

(b) Two or more dissenting limited partners may join as plaintiffs or be joined as defendants in any such action and two or more such actions may be consolidated.

(c) On the trial of the action, the court shall determine the issues. If the status of the limited partnership interest as a dissenting interest is in issue, the court shall first determine that issue. If the fair market value of the dissenting interest is in issue, the court shall determine, or shall appoint one or more impartial appraisers to determine, the fair market value of the dissenting interest.

## California Code Comment
*By Phil Jelsma*

Source: **Cal Corp Code Section 15679.6.**

## SECTION 15911.26. APPRAISAL OF FAIR MARKET VALUE OF LIMITED PARTNERSHIP INTEREST; JUDGMENT; PAYMENT; COSTS.

(a) If the court appoints an appraiser or appraisers, they shall proceed forthwith to determine the fair market value per interest of the outstanding limited partnership interests of the limited partnership, by class if necessary. Within the time fixed by the court, the appraisers, or a majority of them, shall make and file a report in the office of the clerk of the court. Thereupon, on the motion of any party, the report shall be submitted to the court and considered on such additional evidence as the court considers relevant. If the court finds the report reasonable, the court may confirm it.

(b) If a majority of the appraisers appointed fails to make and file a report within 30 days from the date of their appointment, or within such further time as may be allowed by the court, or the report is not confirmed by the court, the court shall determine the fair market value per interest of the outstanding limited partnership interests of the limited partnership, by class if necessary.

(c) Subject to Section 15911.27, judgment shall be rendered against the limited partnership for payment of an amount equal to the fair market value, as determined by the court, of each dissenting interest which any dissenting limited partner who is a party, or has intervened, is entitled to require the limited partnership to purchase, with interest thereon at the legal rate on judgments from the date of consummation of the reorganization.

(d) Any such judgment shall be payable forthwith, provided, however, that with respect to limited partnership interests evidenced by transferable certificates of interest, only upon the endorsement and delivery to the limited partnership of those certificates representing the interests described in the judgment. Any party may appeal from the judgment.

(e) The costs of the action, including reasonable compensation for the appraisers, to be fixed by the court, shall be assessed or apportioned as the court considers equitable, but, if the appraisal exceeds the price offered by the limited partnership, the limited partnership shall pay the costs (including, in the discretion of the court, if the value awarded by the court for the dissenting interest is more than 125 percent of the price offered by the limited partnership under subdivision (a) of Section 15911.05, attorneys' fees and fees of expert witnesses).

### California Code Comment
*By Phil Jelsma*

Source: **Cal Corp Code Section 15679.7.**

**SECTION 15911.27. WITHHOLDING OF CERTAIN PAYMENTS DUE TO DISSENTING LIMITED PARTNERS.** To the extent that the payment to dissenting limited partners of the fair market value of their dissenting interests would require the dissenting limited partners to return such payment or a portion thereof by reason of Section 15905.09 or the Uniform Fraudulent Transfer Act (Chapter 1 (commencing with Section 3439) of Title 2 of Part 2 of Division 4 of the Civil Code), then that payment or portion thereof shall not be made and the dissenting limited partners shall become creditors of the limited partnership for the amount not paid, together with interest thereon at the legal rate on judgments until the date of payment, but subordinate to all other creditors in any proceeding relating to the winding up and dissolution of the limited partnership, such debt to be payable when permissible.

### California Code Comment
*By Phil Jelsma*

Source: **Cal Corp Code Section 15679.8.**

**SECTION 15911.28. CASH DISTRIBUTIONS CREDITED AGAINST AMOUNT TO BE PAID FOR DISSENTING INTEREST.** Any cash distributions made by a limited partnership to a dissenting limited partner after the date of consummation of the reorganization, but prior to any payment by the limited partnership for such dissenting limited partner's interest, shall be credited against the total amount to be paid by the limited partnership for such dissenting interest.

**California Code Comment**
*By Phil Jelsma*

Source: **Cal Corp Code Section 15679.9.**

**SECTION 15911.29. RIGHTS AND PRIVILEGES OF DIS-SENTING LIMITED PARTNERS; NO RIGHT TO WITH-DRAWAL OF DEMAND FOR PAYMENT.** Except as expressly limited by this article, dissenting limited partners shall continue to have all the rights and privileges incident to their interests immediately prior to the reorganization, including limited liability, until payment by the limited partnership for their dissenting interests. A dissenting limited partner may not withdraw a demand for payment unless the limited partnership consents thereto.

**California Code Comment**
*By Phil Jelsma*

Source: **Cal Corp Code Section 15679.10.**

**SECTION 15911.30. LOSS OF STATUS AS DISSENTING IN-TEREST.** A dissenting interest loses its status as a dissenting interest and the holder thereof ceases to be a dissenting limited partner and ceases to be entitled to require the limited partnership to purchase the interest upon the happening of any of the following:

(a) The limited partnership abandons the reorganization. Upon abandonment of the reorganization, the limited partnership shall pay, on demand, to any dissenting limited partner who has initiated proceeding in good faith under this article, all reasonable expenses incurred in such proceedings and reasonable attorneys' fees.

(b) The interest is transferred prior to its submission for endorsement in accordance with Section 15911.23.

(c) The dissenting limited partner and the limited partnership do not agree upon the status of the interest as a dissenting interest or upon the purchase price of the dissenting interest, and neither files a complaint nor intervenes in a pending action, as provided in Section 15911.25, within six months after the date upon which notice of the approval of the reorganization by the requisite vote or consent of limited partners was mailed to the limited partner.

(d) The dissenting limited partner, with the consent of the limited partnership, withdraws such limited partner's demand for purchase of the dissenting interest.

California Code Comment
By Phil Jelsma

Source: Cal Corp Code Section 15679.11.

## SECTION 15911.31. SUSPENSION OF PROCEEDINGS PENDING OUTCOME OF LITIGATION.

If litigation is instituted to test the sufficient or regularity of the vote or consent of the limited partners in authorizing a reorganization, any proceedings under Sections 15911.25 and 15911.26 shall be suspended until final determination of that litigation.

California Code Comment
By Phil Jelsma

Source: Cal Corp Code Section 15679.12.

## SECTION 15911.32. LIMITED PARTNERSHIPS AND PARTNERSHIPS SUBJECT TO ARTICLE.

(a) This article applies to the following:

(1) A domestic limited partnership formed on or after January 1, 1991.

(2) A foreign limited partnership if (A) the foreign limited partnership was formed on or after January 1, 1991 or filed an application to qualify to do business on or after January 1, 1991, and (B) limited partners holding more than 50 percent of the voting power held by all limited partners of the foreign limited partnership reside in this state.

(3) A limited partnership if the partnership agreement so provides or if all general partners and a majority in interest of the limited partners determine that this article shall apply.

(b) This article does not apply to limited partnership interests governed by limited partnership agreements whose terms and provisions specifically set forth the amount to be paid in respect of such interests in the event of a reorganization of the limited partnership, or to limited partnerships with 35 or fewer limited partners, unless the partnership agreement provides that this article shall apply or unless all general partners and a majority in interest of the limited partners agree that this article shall apply.

## California Code Comment
*By Phil Jelsma*

Source: **Cal Corp Code Section 15679.13**.

## SECTION 15911.33. RIGHTS OF LIMITED PARTNERS TO CHALLENGE REORGANIZATION.

(a) No limited partner of a limited partnership who has a right under this article to demand payment of cash for the interest owned by such limited partner in a limited partnership shall have any right at law or in equity to attack the validity of the reorganization, or to have the reorganization set aside or rescinded, except in an action to test whether the vote or consent of limited partners required to authorize or approve the reorganization has been obtained in accordance with the procedures established therefor by the partnership agreement of the limited partnership.

(b) If one of the parties to a reorganization is directly or indirectly controlled by, or under common control with, another party to the reorganization, subdivision (a) shall not apply to any limited partner of such controlled party who has not demanded payment of cash for such limited partner's interest pursuant to this article; but if such limited partner institutes any action to attack the validity of the reorganization or to have the reorganization set aside or rescinded, the limited partner shall not thereafter have any right to demand payment of cash for such limited partner's interest pursuant to this article.

(c) If one of the parties to a reorganization is directly or indirectly controlled by, or under common control with, another party to the reorganization, then, in any action to attack the validity of the reorganization or to have the reorganization set aside or rescinded, (1) a party to a reorganization which controls another party to a reorganization shall have the burden of proving that the transaction is just and reasonable as to the limited partners of the controlled party, and (2) a person who controls two or more parties to a reorganization shall have the burden of proving that the transaction is just and reasonable as to the limited partners of any party so controlled.

(d) Subdivisions (b) and (c) shall not apply if a majority in interest of the limited partners other than limited partners who are directly or indirectly controlled by, or under common control with, another party to the reorganization approve or consent to the reorganization.

(e) This section shall not prevent a partner of a limited partnership that is a party to a reorganization from bringing an action against a general partner of the limited partnership, the limited partnership, or any person controlling a general partner at law or in equity as to any matters (including, without limitation, an action for breach of fiduciary obligation or fraud) other than to attack the validity of the reorganization or to have the reorganization set aside or rescinded.

### California Code Comment
*By Phil Jelsma*

Source: **Cal Corp Code Section 15679.14**.

## ARTICLE 12.
## MISCELLANEOUS PROVISIONS

**SECTION 15912.01. UNIFORMITY OF APPLICATION AND CONSTRUCTION.** In applying and construing this chapter, consideration must be given to the need to promote uniformity of the law with respect to its subject matter among states that enact it.

**SECTION 15912.02. SEVERABILITY CLAUSE.** If any provision of this chapter or its application to any person or circumstance is held invalid, the invalidity does not affect other provisions or applications of this chapter which can be given effect without the invalid provision or application, and to this end, the provisions of this chapter are severable.

**SECTION 15912.03. RELATION TO ELECTRONIC SIGNATURES IN GLOBAL AND NATIONAL COMMERCE ACT.** This chapter modifies, limits, or supersedes the federal Electronic Signatures in Global and National Commerce Act, 15 U.S.C. Section 7001 *et seq.,* but this chapter does not modify, limit, or supersede Section 101(c) of that act or authorize electronic delivery of any of the notices described in Section 103(b) of that act.

**SECTION 15912.04. EFFECTIVE DATE.** This chapter shall become operative on January 1, 2008.

### Uniform Limited Partnership Act Comment

Section 15912.06 specifies how this chapter affects domestic limited partnerships, with special provisions pertaining to domestic limited partnerships formed before the chapter's effective date. Section 15912.06 contains no comparable provisions for foreign limited partnerships. Therefore, once this chapter is effective, it applies immediately to all foreign limited partnerships, whether formed before or after the chapter's effective date.

## SECTION 15912.06. APPLICATION TO EXISTING RELATIONSHIPS.

(a) Before January 1, 2010, this chapter governs only:

(1) a limited partnership formed on or after January 1, 2008; and

(2) except as otherwise provided in subdivisions (c) and (d), a limited partnership formed before January 1, 2008 which elects, in the manner provided in its partnership agreement or by law for amending the partnership agreement, to be subject to this chapter.

(b) Except as otherwise provided in subdivision (c), on and after January 1, 2010, this chapter governs all limited partnerships.

(c) With respect to a limited partnership formed before January 1, 2008, the following rules apply except as the partners otherwise elect in the manner provided in the partnership agreement or by law for amending the partnership agreement:

(1) Section 15901.04(c) does not apply and the limited partnership has whatever duration it had under the law applicable immediately before January 1, 2008.

(2) Sections 15906.01 and 15906.02 do not apply and a limited partner has the same right and power to dissociate from the limited partnership, with the same consequences, as existed immediately before January 1, 2008.

(3) Subdivision (d) of Section 15906.03 does not apply.

(4) Subdivision (e) of Section 15906.03 does not apply and a court has the same power to expel a general partner as the court had immediately before January 1, 2008.

(5) Subdivision (c) of Section 15908.01 does not apply and the connection between a person's dissociation as a general partner and the dissolution of the limited partnership is the same as existed immediately before January 1, 2008.

(d) With respect to a limited partnership that elects pursuant to paragraph (2) of subdivision (a) to be subject to this chapter, after the election takes effect the provisions of this chapter relating to the liability of the limited partnership's general partners to third parties apply:

(1) before January 1, 2010, to:

(A) a third party that had not done business with the limited partnership in the year before the election took effect; and

(B) a third party that had done business with the limited partnership in the year before the election took effect only if the third party knows or has received a notification of the election; and

(2) on and after January 1, 2010, to all third parties, but those provisions remain inapplicable to any obligation incurred while those provisions were inapplicable under subparagraph (B) of paragraph (1).

**SECTION 15912.07. PRIOR ACTIONS.** This chapter does not affect an action commenced, proceeding brought, or right accrued before this chapter becomes operative.

### Uniform Limited Partnership Act Comment

**Source:** RUPA Section 1206.

This section pertains exclusively to domestic limited partnerships—*i.e.,* to limited partnerships formed under this chapter or a predecessor statute enacted by the same jurisdiction. For foreign limited partnerships, see the Comment to Section 15912.04.

This chapter governs all limited partnerships formed on or after the chapter's effective date. As for pre-existing limited partnerships, this section establishes an optional "elect in" period and a mandatory, all-inclusive date. The "elect in" period runs from the effective date, stated in Section 15912.04, until the all-inclusive date, stated in both subdivision(a) and (b).

During the "elect in" period, a pre-existing limited partnership may elect to become subject to this chapter. Subsection (d) states certain important consequences for a limited partnership that elects in. Beginning on the all-inclusive date, each pre-existing limited partnership that has not previously elected in becomes subject to this chapter by operation of law.

**Subsection (c)**—This subdivision specifies six provisions of this chapter which never automatically apply to any pre-existing limited partnership. Except for subdivision (c)(2), the list refers to provisions governing the relationship of the partners inter se and considered too different than predecessor law to be fairly applied to a preexisting limited partnership without the consent of its partners. Each of these inter se provisions is subject to change in the partnership agreement. However, many pre-existing limited partnerships may have taken for granted the analogous provisions of predecessor law and may therefore not have addressed the issues in their partnership agreements.

**Subsection (c)(1)**—Section 15901.04(c) provides that a limited partnership has a perpetual duration.

**Subsection (c)(2)** -Section 15906.01 and 15906.02 concern a person's dissociation as a limited partner.

**Subsection (c)(3)**—Section 15906.03(4) provides for the expulsion of a general partner by the unanimous consent of the other partners in specified circumstances.

**Subsection (c)(4)**—Section 15906.03(5) provides for the expulsion of a general partner by a court in specified circumstances.

**Subsection (c)(5)**—Section 15908.01(3) concerns the continuance or dissolution of a limited partnership following a person's dissociation as a general partner.

**Subsection (d)**—Following RUPA Section 1206(c), this subdivision limits the efficacy of the chapter's liability protections for partners of an "electing in" limited partnership. The limitation:

applies only to the benefit of "a third party that had done business with the limited partnership in the year before the election took effect," and

ceases to apply when "the third party knows or has received a notification of the election" or on the "all-inclusive" date, whichever occurs first.

If the limitation causes a provision of this chapter to be inapplicable with regard to a third party, the comparable provision of predecessor law applies.

Example: A pre-existing limited partnership elects to be governed by this chapter before the "all-inclusive" date. Two months before the election, Third Party provided services to the limited partnership. Third Party neither knows nor has received a notification of the election. Until the "all inclusive" date, with regard to Third Party, Section 303's full liability shield does not apply to each limited partner. Instead, each limited partner has the liability shield applicable under predecessor law.

**Subsection (d)(2)**—To the extent subdivision (d) causes a provision of this chapter to be inapplicable when an obligation is incurred, the inapplicability continues as to that obligation even after the "all inclusive" date.

# CORRELATION TABLES FOR THE UNIFORM LIMITED PARTNERSHIP ACT OF 2008 (Re-RULPA)

The Uniform Limited Partnership Act of 2008 (Re-RULPA) (Corp C §§15900–15912.07), operative January 1, 2008, applies to limited partnerships in three stages:

- Limited partnerships formed before January 1, 2008, may elect to be covered. Corp C §15912.06(a)(2); but see Corp C §15912.06(c), (d).

- All limited partnerships formed on or after January 1, 2008. Corp C §15912.06(a)(1).

- All limited partnerships on or after January 1, 2010. Corp C §15912.06(b); but see Corp C §15912.06(c).

Re-RULPA is a stand-alone act, de-linked from both the existing California Revised Limited Partnership Act (CRLPA) (Corp C §§15611–15724), and the Uniform Partnership Act of 1994 (RUPA) (Corp C §§16100–16962), both of which formerly governed limited partnerships. It is modeled on the national Uniform Limited Partnership Act. For this reason, it is not always possible to draw a direct one-to-one correlation between a former provision and a new provision or a new provision and a former one.

Unique features in Re-RULPA include those involving a certificate of revival (see Corp C §15902.09) and those eliminating fiduciary duties for limited partners (see Corp C §15903.05(a)).

To assist in determining which provisions of Re-RULPA apply in any particular situation involving a client's limited partnership, two correlation tables are included here:

**Table 1**. This table converts, to the extent feasible, from the existing California Limited Partnership Act (CRLPA) to new provisions of Re-RULPA. CRLPA will be repealed as of January 1, 2010. Corp C §15724.

**Table 2**. This table correlates new Re-RULPA provisions to existing statutes, which may be. found in CRLPA as well as other locations in the Corporations Code.

## CORRELATION TABLE 1
## UNIFORM LIMITED PARTNERSHIP ACT OF 2008 (Re-RULPA)
## OLD TO NEW (CRLPA TO RE-RULPA)

| CRLPA | Summary of CRLPA Provision | Uniform Limited Partnership Act of 2008 (Re-RULPA) |
|---|---|---|
| §15611 | Definitions | §§15901.02, 15911.01 |
| §15612 | Name of limited partnership | §15901.08 |
| §15613 | Reservation of name certificate | §15901.09 |
| §15614 | Agent, office for service of process | §15901.14 |
| §15615 | Books and records to be kept | §15901.11 |
| §15616 | Type of business | §15901.04 |
| §15617 | Partner's transactions with partnership | §15901.12 |
| §15618 | Statutes may be varied by agreement | §15901.10(b) |
| §15619 | Enforceability of breach of agreement provisions | §15905.02(d) |
| §15620 | Effective date and resubmission of filed documents | §15902.06(c), (d) |
| §15621 | Partnership agreement | §15902.01 |
| §15622 | Amending certificate of partnership | §15902.02 |
| §15623 | Certificate of dissolution, cancellation, or continuation | §15902.03 |
| §15624 | Executing certificate | §§15902.04, 15902.08 |

| CRLPA | Summary of CRLPA Provision | Uniform Limited Partnership Act of 2008 (Re-RULPA) |
|---|---|---|
| §15625 | Failure to execute or file certificate | §15902.05 |
| §15626 | Filing certificate of amendment | §§15902.02, 15902.03 |
| §15627 | Service of process | §15901.16 |
| §15627.5 | Jurisdiction | §15901.17 |
| §15628 | Filing with Secretary of State | §15902.06 |
| §15631 | Admitting additional limited partners | §15903.01 |
| §15631.5 | Classes of limited partners | §15903.07 |
| §15632 | Liability of limited partners | §§15903.02, 15903.03 |
| §15633 | Liability of presumed, good faith limited partner | §15903.06 |
| §15634 | Limited partners' right to information | §15903.04, 15904.07(h) |
| §15635 | Attorney General actions for failure to comply with §15634 | See Comment to §15903.02 |
| §15636 | Rights and duties of limited partners | §15901.15 |
| §15637 | Meetings of partners | |
| §15638 | Certificate of interest in partnership | |
| §15641 | Admitting additional general partners | §15904.01 |
| §15642 | When person ceases to be general partner | See §15906.03 |
| §15643 | Rights and powers of general partner | §§15904.02(a), 15904.04, 15904.06 |
| §15644 | Contribution by general partner | §15901.13 |

| CRLPA | Summary of CRLPA Provision | Uniform Limited Partnership Act of 2008 (Re-RULPA) |
|---|---|---|
| §15645 | Classes of general partners | §15904.09 |
| §15651 | Contribution not necessary to become partner | |
| §15652 | Claims against partnership | |
| §15653 | Allocating profits and losses | §15905.035 |
| §15654 | Distributions of money or property | §15905.03 |
| §15655 | Obligation to contribute cash or perform services | §15905.02(a) |
| §15661 | Entitlement to interim distributions | |
| §15662 | General partner's withdrawal | |
| §15663 | Limited partner's withdrawal | |
| §15664 | Distributions on withdrawal | |
| §15665 | Partner's status as creditor | §15905.07 |
| §15666 | When partner is obligated to return distribution | §§15905.08, 15905.09 |
| §15671 | Limited partnership interest as personal property | |
| §15672 | Assigning or encumbering partnership interest | §15907.02 |
| §15673 | Creditor rights | §15907.03 |
| §15674 | Assignee may become limited partner | §15907.02(h) |
| §15675 | Deceased or incompetent limited partner | §15907.04 |
| §15677.1 | Definitions | §15911.01 |

| CRLPA | Summary of CRLPA Provision | Uniform Limited Partnership Act of 2008 (Re-RULPA) |
|---|---|---|
| §15677.2 | Conversion to foreign business entity | §15911.02 |
| §15677.3 | Conversion plan | §15911.03 |
| §15677.4 | Effective date of conversion | §15911.04 |
| §15677.5 | Complying with foreign laws | §15911.05 |
| §15677.6 | Certificate of conversion | §15911.06 |
| §15677.7 | Effect on real property | §15911.07 |
| §15677.8 | Converting to domestic limited partnership | §15911.08 |
| §15677.9 | Effect of conversion | §15911.09 |
| §15678.1 | What entities may merge | §§15911.10, 15911.11 |
| §15678.2 | Agreement of merger | §15911.12 |
| §15678.3 | Commissioner's approval | §15911.13 |
| §15678.4 | Certificate of merger | §15911.14 |
| §15678.5 | Effective date of merger | §15911.15 |
| §15678.6 | Surviving limited partnership | §15911.16 |
| §15678.7 | Foreign limited partnership merging with domestic limited partnership | §15911.17 |
| §15678.8 | Real property rights on merger | §15911.18 |
| §15678.9 | Recording certificate of merger | §15911.19 |
| §15678.10 | Assuming tax liability | |

| CRLPA | Summary of CRLPA Provision | Uniform Limited Partnership Act of 2008 (Re-RULPA) |
|---|---|---|
| §15679.1 | Definitions of "reorganization" and "control" | §15911.20 |
| §15679.2 | Purchasing interests of dissenting partnerships | §15911.21 |
| §15679.3 | Notice of approval of reorganization by outstanding interests | §15911.22 |
| §15679.4 | Notice of number of interests demanded to be purchased | §15911.23 |
| §15679.5 | Agreements on fair market value of dissenting interests | §15911.24 |
| §15679.6 | Denying status as dissenting interest | §15911.25 |
| §15679.7 | Appraisals | §15911.26 |
| §15679.8 | Effect of Uniform Fraudulent Transfer Act on payment to dissenters. | §15911.27 |
| §15679.9 | Cash distributions to dissenting partner | §15911.28 |
| §15679.10 | Rights of dissenting limited partners | §15911.29 |
| §15679.11 | Loss of status as dissenting interest | §15911.30 |
| §15679.12 | Effect of litigation | §15911.31 |
| §15679.13 | Application of this article | §15911.32 |
| §15679.14 | Right to challenge validity of reorganization | §15911.33 |
| §15681 | Nonjudicial dissolution | §15908.01 |
| §15682 | Judicial dissolution | §15908.02 |
| §15683 | Winding up on dissolution | §15908.03 |
| §15684 | Distributing assets | §15908.09(a) |

| CRLPA | Summary of CRLPA Provision | Uniform Limited Partnership Act of 2008 (Re-RULPA) |
|---|---|---|
| §15685 | Binding partnership on dissolution | §15908.04 |
| §15691 | Governing law | §15909.01 |
| §15692 | Registration | §15909.02 |
| §15693 | Issuing certificate of registration | §§15909.02, 15909.04, 15909.05 |
| §15694 | Rights of limited partners residing in state | |
| §15695 | Amending application for registration | §15909.06 |
| §15696 | Cancelling registration | §15909.07 |
| §15697 | Transacting business without registration | §15909.07(e) |
| §15698 | Attorney General enforcement | §15909.08 |
| §15699 | Foreign lending institutions | |
| §15701 | Class actions | |
| §15702 | Derivative actions | §15910.02 |
| §§15710–15714 | Transition provisions | §§15912.04–15912.07 |
| §15721 | Title of act | §15900 |
| §15722 | General partnership law governs any case not covered by CRLPA | |
| §15723 | Provisions may be added, altered, or repealed | |
| §15724 | Repeal of CRLPA on 1/1/2010 | |

**CORRELATION TABLE 2**

**UNIFORM LIMITED PARTNERSHIP ACT OF 2008 (Re-RULPA)**

**NEW TO OLD (Re-RULPA TO FORMER CORPORATIONS CODE)**

| Uniform Limited Partnership Act of 2008 (Re-RULPA) | Summary | Former Corporations Code Section |
|---|---|---|
| **ARTICLE I: GENERAL PROVISIONS** | | |
| §15900 | Name of Act | §15721 |
| §15901.02 | Definitions | §15611 |
| §15901.02(a) | Definition of "acknowledged" | §15611(a) |
| §15901.02(b) | Definition of "certificate of limited partnership" | §15611(c) |
| §15901.02(c) | Definition of "contribution" | §15611(g) |
| §15901.02(d) | Definition of "debtor in bankruptcy" | §16101(2) |
| §15901.02(e) | Definition of "designated office" | |
| §15901.02(f) | Definition of "distribution" | §15611(j) |
| §15901.02(g) | Definition of "domestic corporation" | §15611(k) |
| §15901.02(h) | Definition of "electronic transmission by partnership" | §16101(4) |
| §15901.02(i) | Definition of "electronic transmission to partnership" | §16101(5) |
| §15901.02(j) | Definition of "foreign limited liability limited partnership" | §16101(6) |
| §15901.02(k) | Definition of "foreign limited partnership" | §15611(l) |

| Uniform Limited Partnership Act of 2008 (Re-RULPA) | Summary | Former Corporations Code Section |
|---|---|---|
| §15901.02(l) | Definition of "foreign other business entity" | §15611(m) |
| §15901.02(m) | Definition of "general partner" | §15611(n) |
| §15901.02(n) | Definition of "interests of all partners" | §15611(o) |
| §15901.02(o) | Definition of "interests of limited partners" | §15611(p) |
| §15901.02(p) | Definition of "limited partner" | §15611(q) |
| §15901.02(q) | Definition of "limited partnership or domestic limited partnership" | §15611(r) |
| §15901.02(r) | Definition of "mail" | §15611(s) |
| §15901.02(s) | Definition of majority in interest of all partners" | §15611(t) |
| §15901.02(t) | Definition of "majority in interest of the limited partners" | §15611(u) |
| §15901.02(u) | Definition of "other business entity" | §15611(v) |
| §15901.02(v) | Definition of "parent" | §15611(w) |
| §15901.02(w) | Definition of "partner" | §15611(x) |
| §15901.02(x) | Definition of "partnership agreement" | §15611(y) |
| §15901.02(y) | Definition of "person" | §15611(z) |
| §15901.02(z) | Definition of "person dissociated as general partner" | |
| §15901.02(aa) | Definition of "principal office" | |

| Uniform Limited Partnership Act of 2008 (Re-RULPA) | Summary | Former Corporations Code Section |
|---|---|---|
| §15901.02(ab) | Definition of "proxy" | §15611(aa) |
| §15901.02(ac) | Definition of "record" | |
| §15901.02(ad | Definition of "required information" | |
| §15901.02(ae) | Definition of "return of capital" | §15611(ab) |
| §15901.02(af) | Definition of "sign" | |
| §15901.02(ag) | Definition of "state" | §§15611(ac), 16101(16) |
| §15901.02(ah) | Definition of "time a notice is given or sent" | §15611(af) |
| §15901.02(ai) | Definition of "transact intrastate business" | §15611(ag) |
| §15901.02(aj) | Definition of "transfer" | §16101(18) |
| §15901.02(ak) | Definition of "transferable interest" | §16502 |
| §15901.02(al) | Definition of "transferee" | |
| §15901.03 | Knowledge, notice, receipt of notification | §16102 |
| §15901.04 | Nature, purpose, and duration of entity | |
| §15901.04(a) | Limited partnership as distinct from partners | §16201 |
| §15901.04(b) | Any lawful purpose, except banking, insurance, trust company | §15616 |
| §15901.04(c) | Perpetual duration | |
| §15901.05 | No limit to powers, except right to sue, be sued, defend | §16307 |

| Uniform Limited Partnership Act of 2008 (Re-RULPA) | Summary | Former Corporations Code Section |
|---|---|---|
| §15901.06 | California law governs | §16106(a) |
| §15901.07 | Law and equity; interest rate | §16104 |
| §15901.08 | Name of limited partnership | §15612 |
| §15901.09 | Name reservation | §15613 |
| §15901.10 | Partnership agreement; limitations | §16103 |
| §15901.10(a) | Partnership agreement or Act governs | §16103(a) |
| §15901.10(b) | Partnership agreement limitations | §§15618, 16103(b) |
| §15901.11 | Records to be maintained at designated office | §15615 |
| §15901.11(1) | List of general and limited partners | §15615(a) |
| §15901.11(2) | Copy of limited partnership certificate | §15615(b) |
| §15901.11(3) | Copy of certificate of merger or consolidation | |
| §15901.11(4) | Copy of tax returns | §15615(c) |
| §15901.11(5) | Copy of partnership agreement | §15615(d) |
| §15901.11(6) | Copy of financial statements | §15615(e) |
| §15901.11(7) | Record of consents, if record made | |
| §15901.11(8) | Records of contributions, transferable interests, dissolution events | |

| Uniform Limited Partnership Act of 2008 (Re-RULPA) | Summary | Former Corporations Code Section |
|---|---|---|
| §15901.12 | Rights of partner transacting business with limited partnership | §15617 |
| §15901.13 | Person may be general and limited partner | §15644 |
| §15901.14 | Office and agent for service of process | §15614 |
| §15901.14(a) | Designation of office and agent | §15614(a) |
| §15901.14(b) | Foreign limited partnership must designate agent | §§15614(b), 15692© |
| §15901.14(c) | Requirements for agent | §15627(d) |
| §15901.15 | Action without meeting; proxy | §15637(i), (j) |
| §15901.16 | Service of process | §15627 |
| §15901.17 | Consent to jurisdiction, arbitration, and service by legal process | §15627.5 |
| **ARTICLE 2: FORMATION, CERTIFICATE OF LIMITED PARTNERSHIP AND OTHER FILINGS** | | |
| §15902.01 | Certificate of limited partnership | §15621 |
| §15902.01(a) | Required contents of certificate | §15621(a)(1)–(4) |
| §15902.01(b) | Certificate may contain other matters | §15521(a)(5) |
| §15902.01(c) | Limited partnership formed when Secretary of State files certificate | §15621(b) |

| Uniform Limited Partnership Act of 2008 (Re-RULPA) | Summary | Former Corporations Code Section |
|---|---|---|
| §15902.01(d) | Inconsistencies between partnership agreement and certificate | |
| §15902.01(e) | Recording certificate | §15621(d) |
| §15902.01(f) | Certificate may be cancelled for non-payment of fee | §15621(e) |
| §15902.01(g) | Notice of annual tax | §15621(f) |
| §15902.02 | Amendment of certificate | §§15622, 15626 |
| §15902.02(a) | Amendment filed with Secretary of State; contents | §15622(a) |
| §15902.02(b) | Prompt filing required on occurrence of certain events | §15622(b) |
| §15902.02(c) | Prompt filing required after general partner discovers falsity | §15622(b)(6) |
| §15902.02(d) | Optional amendment at any time | §15622(d) |
| §15902.02(e) | Restated certificate may be filed; contents | §15622(e) |
| §15902.02(f) | Effective when filed | |
| §15902.03 | Certificate of cancellation; contents | §§15623(b), 15626+C266 |
| §15902.04 | Signature requirements for forms | §15624 |
| §15902.04(a)(1) | Certificate of limited partnership | §15624(a)(1) |
| §15902.04(a)(2)–(4) | Certificate of amendment | §15624(a)(2) |
| §15902.04(a)(5) | Restated certificate | §15624(a)(8) |
| §15902.04(a)(6) | Certificate of cancellation | §15624(a)(4) |

| Uniform Limited Partnership Act of 2008 (Re-RULPA) | Summary | Former Corporations Code Section |
|---|---|---|
| §15902.04(a)(7) | Certificate of conversion | §15677.6(b) |
| §15902.04(a)(8) | Certificate of merger | §15624(a)(6) |
| §15902.04(a)(9) | Any other record for limited partnership | |
| §15902.04(a)(10) | Certificate of dissociation | §16704 |
| §15902.04(a)(11) | Certificate of withdrawal | |
| §15902.04(a)(12) | Record for foreign limited partnership | |
| §15902.04(a)(13) | Any other record for foreign limited partnership | |
| §15902.04(b) | Attorney in fact | §15624(b) |
| §15902.04(c) | Secretary not required to verify status | |
| §15902.05 | Failure to sign records properly | §15625 |
| §15902.06 | Mandatory forms | §15620 |
| §15902.06(a) | Form and fee to be delivered to Secretary of State | §15628 |
| §15902.06(b) | Effective date; delayed effective date | §15628 |
| §15902.06(c) | Revocation before effective date | §15620(a) |
| §15902.06(d) | Resubmission; written opinion | §15620(b) |
| §15902.07 | Certificate of correction | |
| §15902.08 | False information in filing | §15624(c)–(f) |

| Uniform Limited Partnership Act of 2008 (Re-RULPA) | Summary | Former Corporations Code Section |
|---|---|---|
| §15902.09 | Certificate of revival | |
| **ARTICLE 3: LIMITED PARTNERS** | | |
| §15903.01 | Becoming limited partner | §15631 |
| §15903.02 | Limited partner cannot bind or act for partnership | §15632 |
| §15903.03 | Limited partner's liability and participation | §15632 |
| §15903.04 | Limited partner's inspection, copying rights | §15634 |
| §15903.04(a) | Inspection of information required to be maintained | §15634(a), (b) |
| §15903.04(b) | Inspection of information on state of limited partnership | §16403 |
| §15903.04(c) | Response to demand under (b) | |
| §15903.04(d) | Right of dissociated limited partner to inspect | §16403 |
| §15903.04(e) | Response to demand under (c) | |
| §15903.04(f) | Right to inspect on death of limited partner | |
| §15903.04(g) | Limits on inspection rights for trade secrets and confidential information | |
| §15903.04(h) | Limited partnership may impose reasonable restrictions on use of information | |
| §15903.04(i) | Reasonable costs of copying | |

| Uniform Limited Partnership Act of 2008 (Re-RULPA) | Summary | Former Corporations Code Section |
|---|---|---|
| §15903.04(j) | When consent in issue, limited partnership to provide information to limited partner | §15634(i) |
| §15903.04(k) | Exercising inspection rights through attorney or agent | |
| §15903.04(l) | Rights of persons under legal disability; no inspection rights for transferees | |
| §15903.05 | Limited partner has no fiduciary duty to limited partnership | |
| §15903.06 | Investor's good faith belief in limited partner's status | §15633 |
| §15903.06(a) | No liability for good faith error on making correction or withdrawal | §15633 |
| §15903.06(b) | When investor liable as general partner | §15633(b) |
| §15903.06(c) | Right to withdraw | §15633 |
| §15903.07 | Classes of limited partners; voting | §15631.5 |
| **ARTICLE 4: GENERAL PARTNERS** | | |
| §15904.01 | Becoming general partner | §15641 |
| §15904.02 | Authority of general partner | |
| §15904.02(a) | General partner is agent of limited partnership; authority; binding effect | §15643(a) |
| §15904.02(b) | Act outside ordinary course binds limited partnership if authorized by all other partners | §16301(2) |

| Uniform Limited Partnership Act of 2008 (Re-RULPA) | Summary | Former Corporations Code Section |
|---|---|---|
| §15904.03 | Liability of limited partnership for acts of partner | |
| §15904.04 | Joint and several liability of general partners | §§15643(b); 16306 |
| §15904.05 | Joinder and execution | |
| §15904.05(a) | Joining general partner or suing separately | §16307(a) |
| §15904.05(b) | Judgment against limited partnership not judgment against general partner | §16307© |
| §15904.05(c) | No levy against general partner | §16307(d) |
| §15904.06 | General partner rights in management | §15643(a) |
| §15904.06(a) | Equal rights in management | §15643(a) |
| §15904.06(b) | When consent required | |
| §15904.06(c) | Reimbursement and indemnification | §16401c+C182 |
| §15904.06(d), (e) | Reimbursement of advances; loans | §16401(d), (e) |
| §15904.06(f) | No right to remuneration for services | |
| §15904.07 | General partner inspection, copying rights | |
| §15904.07(a), (b) | General partner inspection rights as to electronic information | §16403 |
| §15904.07(c) | Dissociated general partner's on 10 days' demand | |
| §15904.07(d) | Response within §10 days | |

| Uniform Limited Partnership Act of 2008 (Re-RULPA) | Summary | Former Corporations Code Section |
|---|---|---|
| §15904.07(e) | Death of general partner; rights of representative | |
| §15904.07(f) | Reasonable restrictions on use; burden of proof | |
| §15904.07(g) | Charge reasonable costs | |
| §15904.07(h) | Exercise rights through attorney or agent | §15634(i) |
| §15904.07(i) | Rights not for transferees; exercise by legal representative if legal disability of general partner | |
| §15904.08 | Duties of general partner | |
| §15904.08(a) | Fiduciary duties of loyalty and care | §16404 |
| §15904.08(b) | Duty of loyalty | §16404 |
| §15904.08(c) | Duty of care | §16404 |
| §15904.08(d) | Good faith and fair dealing | §16404 |
| §15904.08(e) | General partner's own interest | |
| §15904.09 | Classes of general partners; voting | §15645 |
| **ARTICLE 5: CONTRIBUTIONS AND DISTRIBUTIONS** | | |
| §15905.01 | Contribution of tangible and intangible property | §15644 |
| §15905.02 | Obligation to contribute | §17201(a)(3) |
| §15905.02(a) | Duty not excused by death, disability, inability | §15655 |

| Uniform Limited Partnership Act of 2008 (Re-RULPA) | Summary | Former Corporations Code Section |
|---|---|---|
| §15905.02(b) | Limited partnership may enforce property contribution in money | |
| §15905.02(c) | Compromise; third party rights | |
| §15905.02(d) | Remedies specified in agreement | §15619 |
| §15905.03 | Distribution on basis of value of contributions | §15654 |
| §15905.035 | Allocation of profits and losses based on agreement | §15653 |
| §15905.04 | Partner has no right to distribution before dissolution | |
| §15905.05 | Person has no right to distribution on dissociation | |
| §15905.06 | Partner has no right to demand non-cash distribution; limited partnership may distribute property by share of distribution | |
| §15905.07 | Partner or transferee has status of creditor; right to offset | §15665 |
| §15905.08 | Limits on distributions | §15666 |
| §15905.08(a) | No distribution in violation of agreement | |
| §15905.08(b) | No distribution if unable to pay debts; liabilities exceed assets | §15666(a) |
| §15905.08(c) | Basis for determining distribution | |
| §15905.08(d) | Date for measuring effect of distribution | |
| §15905.08(e) | Limited partnership debt to general partner has parity with that to unsecured creditors | |

| Uniform Limited Partnership Act of 2008 (Re-RULPA) | Summary | Former Corporations Code Section |
|---|---|---|
| §15905.08(f) | Limited partnership's indebtedness; limitation | |
| §15905.08(g) | Indebtedness issued as distribution | |
| §15905.09 | Liability for improper distribution | §15666 |
| §15905.09(a) | Consenting general partner personally liable to limited partnership to extent of excess | |
| §15905.09(b) | Partner or transferee who knowingly receives improper distribution is liable to limited partnership to extent of excess | |
| §15905.09(c) | General partner may implead and seek contribution | |
| §15905.09(d) | 4 year statute of limitation | §15666(b) |
| **ARTICLE 6: DISSOCIATION** | | |
| §15906.01 | Limited partner right to dissociate | |
| §15906.01(a) | Limited partner has no right to dissociate pre termination | |
| §15906.01(b) | Grounds for dissociation of limited partner | |
| §15906.02 | | |
| §15906.02(a) | Effect of limited partner dissociation | |
| §15906.02(b) | No discharge of preexisting duties | §16703(a) |
| §15906.03 | Grounds for dissociation of general partner | §16601 |
| §15906.04 | General partner's power to dissociate | §16602 |

| Uniform Limited Partnership Act of 2008 (Re-RULPA) | Summary | Former Corporations Code Section |
|---|---|---|
| §15906.04(a) | Express will under §15906.03(a) | |
| §15906.04(b) | Wrongful dissociation | |
| §15906.04(c) | Liability for wrongful dissociation | |
| §15906.05 | General partner dissociation | §15642 |
| §15906.05(a)(1)–(3) | Effect of general partner dissociation | §16603 |
| §15906.05(b) | No discharge of preexisting duties | §16703(a) |
| §15906.06 | Dissociated general partner's power to bind and liability to limited partnership before dissolution | |
| §15906.06(a) | When limited partnership bound by acts of dissociated general partner | §16702(a) |
| §15906.06(b) | When general partner liable to limited partnership for acts while dissociated | §16702(b) |
| §15906.07 | Dissociated general partner's liability to other persons | |
| §15906.07(a) | General partner dissociation not discharge; general partnership personal liability | §16703(a) |
| §15906.07(b) | Liability when general partner dissociation resulted in dissolution | |
| §15906.07(c) | Liability when general partner dissociation did not cause dissolution | |

| Uniform Limited Partnership Act of 2008 (Re-RULPA) | Summary | Former Corporations Code Section |
|---|---|---|
| §15906.07(d), (e) | Release from liability by agreement with creditor | §16703(c), (d) |
| **ARTICLE 7: TRANSFERABLE INTERESTS AND RIGHTS OF TRANSFEREES AND CREDITORS** | | |
| §15907.01 | Partner's transferable interest is personal property | §16502 |
| §15907.02 | Transfer | §§15672, 16503 |
| §15907.02(a) | When transfer permitted | §16503(a) |
| §15907.02(b), (c) | Transferee's rights | §16503(b) |
| §15907.02(d) | Transferor's rights | §16503(d) |
| §15907.02(e) | Limited partnership must have notice of transfer | §16503(e) |
| §15907.02(f) | Transfer in violation of agreement ineffective | §16503(f) |
| §15907.02(g) | Transferee's liability | |
| §15907.02(h) | Transferee as limited partner | §15674 |
| §15907.03 | Charging orders; satisfaction of judgment from debtor's transferable interest | §§15673, 16504 |
| §15907.03(a) | Charging orders | §16504(a) |
| §15907.03(b) | Lien on judgment debtor's transferable interest | §16504(b) |
| §15907.03(c) | Redemption | §16504(c) |

| Uniform Limited Partnership Act of 2008 (Re-RULPA) | Summary | Former Corporations Code Section |
|---|---|---|
| §15907.03(d) | No deprivation of right under exemption laws | §16504(d) |
| §15907.03(e) | Creditor's exclusive remedy | §16504(e) |
| §15907.03(f) | No right to limited partnership property | |
| §15907.04 | Effect of death | §15675 |
| **ARTICLE 8: DISSOLUTION** | | |
| §15908.01 | Nonjudicial dissolution | §15681 |
| §15908.02 | Judicial dissolution | §15682 |
| §15908.02(a) | Dissolution if not reasonably practicable to carry on limited partnership | §15682(a) |
| §15908.02(b), (c) | Avoid dissolution by cash purchase of interests | §17351 |
| §15908.02(d) | 3 disinterested appraisers | §17351 |
| §15908.02(e) | Effect of purchase | §17351 |
| §15908.02(f) | Valuation date | §17351 |
| §15908.03 | Winding up | §15683 |
| §15908.03(a) | Limited partnership continues after dissolution for purpose of winding up | §15683 |
| §15908.03(b) | Powers during winding up | §16803 |
| §15908.03(c) | Person may be appointed to wind up | |

| Uniform Limited Partnership Act of 2008 (Re-RULPA) | Summary | Former Corporations Code Section |
|---|---|---|
| §15908.03(d) | Judicial supervision of winding up | §15683(b) |
| §15908.03(e) | Limited partnerships winding up; limited partnership entitled to compensation | §15683(e) |
| §15908.04 | General partner's power to bind partnership after dissolution | |
| §15908.04(a) | When limited partnership bound by general partner's post-dissolution acts | §15685 |
| §15908.04(b) | When dissociated general partner binds post-dissolution limited partnership | §16702 |
| §15908.05 | Liability of general partner after dissolution | |
| §15908.06 | Handling claims against dissolved limited partnership | |
| §15908.07 | Publishing notice of dissolution | |
| §15908.08 | Barred claims | |
| §15908.09 | Satisfying creditor claims; surplus; insufficiency | |
| §15908.09(a) | Assets to satisfy limited partnership claims | §16807(a) |
| §15908.09(b) | Surplus assets | §16807(a) |
| §15908.09(c) | Insufficient assets | |
| §15908.09(d) | Additional contributions | |
| §15908.09(e) | Estate's liability | §16807(e) |

| Uniform Limited Partnership Act of 2008 (Re-RULPA) | Summary | Former Corporations Code Section |
|---|---|---|
| §15908.09(f) | Enforcement by assignee | §16807(f) |
| **ARTICLE 9: FOREIGN LIMITED PARTNERSHIP** | | |
| §15909.01 | Foreign limited partnership; governing law | §15691 |
| §15909.01(a) | Law of formation | §15691 |
| §15909.01(b) | Certificate cannot be denied based on difference in laws | §15691 |
| §15909.01(c) | No authority to engage in prohibited limited partnership business | |
| §15909.02 | Registration | §§15692, 15693 |
| §15909.02(a) | Contents of form | §15692 |
| §15909.02(b) | Certificate of existence | |
| §15909.03 | Activities that are not "transacting business" in state | §15611(ag) |
| §15909.04 | Filing application; issuing certificate | §15693 |
| §15909.05 | Name requirements; filing fee | §15692(a) |
| §15909.05(a) | No registration if noncomplying name | §15693 |
| §15909.05(b) | Registered foreign limited partnership cannot change to noncomplying name | §15692(a) |
| §15909.05(c) | Secretary of State may cancel for non-payment of fee | §15693 |

| Uniform Limited Partnership Act of 2008 (Re-RULPA) | Summary | Former Corporations Code Section |
|---|---|---|
| §15909.06 | Amending application | §15695 |
| §15909.07 | Cancellation of certificate | §15696 |
| §15909.08 | Attorney General action to restrain | §15698 |
| **ARTICLE 10: ACTIONS BY PARTNERS** | | |
| §15910.01 | Actions by partner | §15636 |
| §15910.01(a) | Direct actions | |
| §15910.01(b) | Proof required | |
| §15910.01(c) | Time limitation determined under other law; right to accounting does not revive barred law claim | |
| §15910.02 | Derivative action; demand required unless futile | §15702 |
| §15910.03 | Partner status required; court hearing; exception | |
| §15910.04 | Complaint must explain demand or futility | §15706 |
| §15910.05 | Proceeds; fees; expenses | §15706 |
| §15910.05(a) | Proceeds belong to limited partnership | |
| §15910.05(b) | Award of fees and expenses to derivative plaintiff | |
| §15910.06 | Grounds for bond | §17501 |

| Uniform Limited Partnership Act of 2008 (Re-RULPA) | Summary | Former Corporations Code Section |
|---|---|---|
| **ARTICLE 11: CONVERSION AND MERGER** | | |
| §15911.01 | Conversion and merger definitions | |
| §15911.01(a) | Definition of "converted entity" | §15677.1(a) |
| §15911.01(b) | Definition of "converted limited partnership" | §15677.1(b) |
| §15911.01(c) | Definition of "converting limited partnership" | §15677.1(c) |
| §15911.01(d) | Definition of "converting entity" | §15677.1(d) |
| §15911.01(e) | Definition of "constituent corporation" | §15611(d) |
| §15911.01(f) | Definition of "constituent limited partnership" | §15611(e) |
| §15911.01(g) | Definition of "constituent other business entity" | §15611(f) |
| §15911.01(h) | Definition of "disappearing limited partnership" | §15611(h) |
| §15911.01(i) | Definition of "disappearing other business entity" | §15611(i) |
| §15911.01(j) | Definition of "foreign other business entity" | §15611(m) |
| §15911.01(k) | Definition of "other business entity" | §15611(v) |
| §15911.01(l) | Definition of "surviving limited partnership" | §15611(ad) |
| §15911.01(m) | Definition of "surviving other business entity" | §15611(ae) |
| §15911.02 | Conversion | §15677.2 |

| Uniform Limited Partnership Act of 2008 (Re-RULPA) | Summary | Former Corporations Code Section |
|---|---|---|
| §15911.02(a) | Bases for conversion | §15677.2(a) |
| §15911.02(b) | Law of converted entity controls | §15677.2(b) |
| §15911.03 | Plan of conversion | §15677.3 |
| §15911.03(a) | Conversion plan requirements | §15677.3(a) |
| §15911.03(b) | Approval requirements | §15677.3(b) |
| §15911.03(c) | Effect of conversion | §15677.3(c) |
| §15911.03(d) | Amending plan | §15677.3(d) |
| §15911.03(e) | Abandoning plan | §15677.3(e) |
| §15911.03(f) | Location of plan | §15677.3(f) |
| §15911.04 | Effective date and evidence of conversion | §15677.4 |
| §15911.04(a) | Effective date of conversion | §15677.4(a) |
| §15911.04(b) | Conclusive evidence | §15677.4(a) |
| §15911.05 | Compliance with other laws and service of process | §15677.5 |
| §15911.05(a) | Conversion into foreign entity | §15677.5(a) |
| §15911.05(b) | Governing law | §15677.5(b) |
| §15911.05(c) | Enforcement of duties | §15677.5(c) |
| §15911.06 | Statement of conversion | §15677.6 |

| Uniform Limited Partnership Act of 2008 (Re-RULPA) | Summary | Former Corporations Code Section |
|---|---|---|
| §15911.06(a) | Required documents | §15677.6(a) |
| §15911.06(b) | Execution; contents | §15677.6(b) |
| §15911.06(c) | Filing operates as certificate of cancellation | §15677.6(c) |
| §15911.07 | Real property | §15677.7 |
| §15911.07(a) | Recording certificate | §15677.7(a) |
| §15911.07(b) | Effect of recording incomplete certificate | §15677.7(b) |
| §15911.07(c) | Conclusive presumption | §15677.7(c) |
| §15911.08 | Conversion to domestic limited partnership | §15677.8 |
| §15911.08(a) | Conversion of other entity to domestic limited partnership; conversion not property transfer | §15677.8(a) |
| §15911.08(b) | Approval of plan of conversion | §15677.8(b) |
| §15911.08(c) | Approval by partners, etc | §15677.8(c) |
| §15911.08(d) | Effective date | §15677.8(d) |
| §15911.09 | Conversion to another entity | §15677.9 |
| §15911.10 | Mergers to be governed by §§15911.11–15911.19 | |
| §15911.11 | Mergers; conditions | §15578.1 |
| §15911.12 | Merger agreement | §15678.2 |

| Uniform Limited Partnership Act of 2008 (Re-RULPA) | Summary | Former Corporations Code Section |
|---|---|---|
| §15911.13 | §15911.12(b) not applicable if commissioner approves terms of transaction | §15678.3 |
| §15911.14 | Surviving entity files certificate of merger; disappearing entity files certificate of satisfaction | §15678.4 |
| §15911.15 | Effective date of merger | §15678.5 |
| §15911.16 | Surviving entity succession to rights, property, and debt of disappearing entity | §15678.6 |
| §15911.17 | Foreign limited partnership merger with domestic entity | §15678.7 |
| §15911.18 | Real property rights; record of ownership | §15678.8 |
| §15911.19 | Recording of certificate | §15678.9 |
| **ARTICLE 11.5: DISSENTING LIMITED PARTNERS' RIGHTS** | | |
| §15911.20 | Definitions concerning dissenting limited partners' rights | §15679.1 |
| §15911.21 | Limited partner right to require purchase of dissenting interest | §15679.2 |
| §15911.22 | Purchase of dissenting interest | §15679.3 |
| §15911.23 | Submission of certificate | §15679.4 |
| §15911.24 | Agreement on purchase; payment | §15679.5 |
| §15911.25 | Complaint within 6 months; multiple dissenting interests | §15679.6 |

| Uniform Limited Partnership Act of 2008 (Re-RULPA) | Summary | Former Corporations Code Section |
|---|---|---|
| §15911.26 | Appraisal | §15679.7 |
| §15911.27 | Effect of limits on distributions | §15679.8 |
| §15911.28 | Cash distributions credited | §15679.9 |
| §15911.29 | Rights of dissenters; no right to withdraw demand for payment without limited partnership consent | §15679.10 |
| §15911.30 | Loss of dissenting partner status | §15679.11 |
| §15911.31 | Suspension of action due to litigation | §15679.12 |
| §15911.32 | Application of statutes | §15679.13 |
| §15911.33 | Limited partner's right to challenge reorganization | §15679.14 |
| **ARTICLE 12: MISCELLANEOUS PROVISIONS** | | |
| §15912.01 | Need for uniformity | §16108 |
| §15912.02 | Severability | §16110 |
| §15912.03 | Effect of federal law | |
| §15912.04 | January 1, 2008 operative date | |
| §15912.06 | Transition provisions | §§15710–15714 |
| §15912.07 | Uniform Limited Partnership Act of 2008 does not affect pre-2008 pending matters | |

CONTINUING EDUCATION OF THE BAR ▪ CALIFORNIA

BU-33919
ISBN 978-0-7626-1366-3